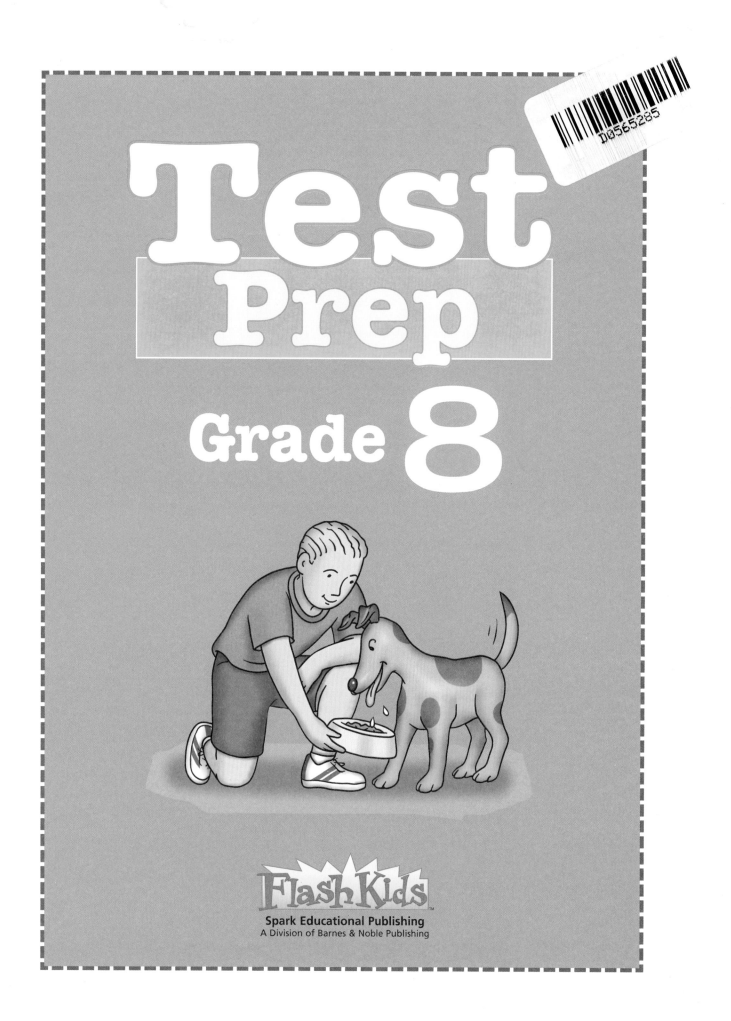

Test Prep

Grade 8

Flash Kids™

Spark Educational Publishing
A Division of Barnes & Noble Publishing

Spark Educational Publishing
A Division of Barnes & Noble Publishing
120 Fifth Avenue
New York, NY 10011

TABLE OF CONTENTS

As you know, standardized tests are an important part of your child's school career. These tests are created by your state's education department and set to its standards of learning for each grade level. These tests are valuable tools that measure how much your child knows in the areas of reading and math. *Test Prep: Grade 8* is designed to familiarize your child with test formats and directions, teach test-taking strategies, and provide practice in skill areas that most states consider important. This workbook will also help your child review the basic skills taught in the eighth grade.

Preparation is the key to helping your child become test-smart. Practicing basic skills in a testing situation can help ensure that your child's scores reflect his or her understanding of the material presented in school. Test-smart students:

- are comfortable in the testing environment;
- know how to approach different kinds of test questions;
- apply knowledge to a variety of test formats;
- use time wisely during tests.

Completing the practice exercises and tests in this workbook can help your child relax and feel ready as test day approaches. This practice also provides a review of the essential skills that will help your child with coursework during the school year.

ABOUT THIS WORKBOOK

Test Prep: Grade 8 is divided into three helpful sections. Practice exercises and mini-tests introduce and review basic test-taking skills. Longer practice tests that mirror the actual tests your child will encounter at school appear at the end of the book.

- **Unit 1: Test-Taking Strategies**

  These pages help your child learn essential strategies to use during any standardized test. You might read these pages together with your child. Talk about which strategies your child has used before and which ones are new.

- **Units 2–7: Mini-Tests**

  Each unit focuses on a subject found on standardized tests: reading comprehension, reading vocabulary, mathematics, problem solving, and language. These mini-tests help your child learn specific test strategies. Each unit concludes with a unit test that covers all of the skills in the unit's lessons.

- **Units 8–11: Practice Tests**

  These longer practice tests help your child apply test-taking skills in a realistic testing environment. Your child will use the Answer Sheet at the back of this book to record responses. Familiarizing your child with the testing experience can lessen feelings of intimidation during any type of school assessment.

Throughout the mini-tests, hints and Test Tips will draw your child's attention to useful ways to approach individual problems. Test Tips do not appear in the final practice tests, which reflect realistic testing situations.

These tests help your child develop four important skills that are crucial in testing situations. Familiarize yourself with these goals in order to support your child's development of these skills.

USING TIME WISELY

All standardized tests are timed. Your child needs to understand how to manage time wisely. Review these strategies together:

- Work rapidly but comfortably.
- Do not spend too much time on any one question.
- Mark items to return to if there is enough time.
- Use any remaining time to review answers.
- Use a watch to keep track of time.

AVOIDING ERRORS

Your child can practice these strategies when choosing the correct answers on standardized tests:

- Pay careful attention to directions.
- Determine what is being asked.
- Mark answers in the appropriate place.
- Check all answers.
- Do not make stray marks on the answer sheet.

REASONING

Standardized tests require your child to think logically when answering each question. These strategies can help your child think through each question before choosing the best answer:

- Before answering a question, read the entire question or passage and all the answer choices.
- Restate questions and answer choices in your own words.
- Use logic and reasoning skills to test answer choices and eliminate incorrect answers.
- Apply skills learned in class and practice situations.

GUESSING

Many standardized tests take away points for incorrect answers. Random guessing will not improve your child's test scores, but educated guessing can help your child score points when the correct answer is not immediately clear.

- Try to answer all of the questions within the allotted time. Do not spend too much time on a question that seems hard.
- Eliminate answers that you know are incorrect. If you cannot do this, skip the question.
- Compare the remaining answers. Restate the question, and then choose the answer that seems most correct.

Daily encouragement and support for learning will help your child feel confident and secure. Every student needs much experience with reading and exposure to a wide variety of reading material. The school curriculum is carefully designed to teach skills your child needs to become a proficient learner. Your home environment is another essential part of the education equation. Here are some ways you can help your child year-round.

CREATE A SUCCESSFUL STUDY SPACE

A quiet, clean, and cheerful study space will help your child develop strong study habits. Provide a study area with an open workspace. Make sure that writing supplies like paper and pencils are nearby, as well as tools like a calculator, ruler, scissors, glue, and a dictionary. You might also create files or boxes to store your child's work. Make separate files for finished works and works in progress. Help your child create and follow a study schedule.

BE A HOMEWORK HELPER

Talk about homework assignments with your child. Your questions can help your child focus on what is important about the task or project. Your interest in schoolwork will encourage your child's enthusiasm and dedication. Check in while your child is working to see if you can answer any questions or help find solutions. Just letting your child know that you care can promote active learning.

USE THE INTERNET EFFECTIVELY

Many eighth graders use the Internet as a reference source. Monitor your child's use of the Internet, and together decide if a Web site probably contains information that is correct. Look for Internet sites sponsored by educational organizations (many of which have URLs that end with .edu). Remind your child that sites written by other students may not have been checked carefully for accuracy. Your child should try to back up important information with library sources, such as encyclopedias and other books.

PRACTICE WITH A CALCULATOR

Many standardized tests allow students to use calculators. Make sure you have a calculator at home that is in good working condition. Calculators do not replace learning math skills. However, using calculators accurately is essential in many real-life situations. Encourage your child to use a calculator to complete homework or to help with household computations.

TALK ABOUT TESTS

Find out from your child's teacher when standardized tests will be given during the school year. Mark the dates on your calendar so that both you and your child know when test day approaches. Try not to schedule big activities for the night before a test.

To prepare for the yearly standardized test, score your child's work in this workbook together. Then talk about questions that were easy, hard, or tricky. Review any items answered incorrectly and work together to understand why another answer is better.

A GOOD NIGHT'S SLEEP

Your child will be more relaxed and alert after a full night of sleep. Some physical exercise before dinner can relieve feelings of stress. Do not place too much emphasis on the upcoming test, but answer any questions your child may have and provide reassurance that your child is ready for the test. Reminders of what to expect may lower anxiety. Help your child choose clothing for the next day, and have it ready so there is no last-minute hunting in the morning.

FOOD FOR THOUGHT

Studies show a direct link between eating a balanced breakfast and student performance. Students who eat a good breakfast are alert in class, concentrate well, and recall information. These skills are useful at any time of the year, but are especially helpful on test day. To make sure your child eats a balanced breakfast, wake up early enough to leave plenty of time for a relaxed meal together.

SUPPORT YOUR CHILD

Remind your child that standardized tests measure learning. They do not measure intelligence. Supportive parents expect their children to do their best. Do not set specific goals or offer rewards for high scores. Instead, assure your child that you will be happy with a positive and wholehearted effort. Doing one's best is what really counts!

AFTER THE TEST

When your child comes home, discuss the testing experience. Do not focus on the test score. Instead, use the opportunity to reassure your child and talk about test-taking strategies. Every test is an opportunity to improve. Ask your child which strategies were especially useful. To keep the mood relaxed at home, choose a fun activity to help your child unwind after the test.

When the test scores arrive, remember to keep the results in perspective. Unless specified, most tests do not measure intelligence. A test score simply measures how well your child knows the materials and skills covered on that specific test.

Be sure to talk about the test score with your child. Remind your child that no single test score gives a complete picture of how much someone knows. Help your child set goals to maintain or improve test scores in the future. Always praise your child for working hard on a test. Test scores might suggest that your child needs improvement in a specific skill or subject. Talk with your child's teacher to find ways to support your child's growth in a particular area.

GET READY FOR TESTS

WHAT ARE STANDARDIZED TESTS?

You will take many different tests while at school. A standardized test is a special test that your state gives to every student in your grade. These tests are designed to find out how much you know about subjects like reading and math. They may not be fun, but they do not have to be a nightmare. This workbook can help you prepare!

WHAT CAN YOU EXPECT ON A STANDARDIZED TEST?

All standardized tests are different, but they do have some things in common.

- **Multiple-Choice Questions**
  Most of these tests use multiple-choice questions. You have to pick the best answer from four or five choices. You usually indicate your choice on an answer sheet by filling in or darkening a circle next to the correct answer.

- **Time Limits**
  Standardized tests all have time limits. It is best to answer as many questions as possible before you run out of time. But do not let the time limit make you nervous. Use it to help you keep going at a good pace.

- **Short Answers and Essays**
  Some standardized tests have questions that require writing an answer. Sometimes the answer is a word or a sentence. Other times you will write a paragraph or an essay. Always read directions carefully to find out how much writing is required.

HOW CAN THIS BOOK HELP?

Everyone gets a little nervous when taking a test. This book can make test-taking easier by providing helpful tips and practice tests. You will learn strategies that will help you find the best answers. You will also review math, reading, and grammar skills that are commonly needed on standardized tests. Here are some hints for using this book.

- Work in a quiet place. When you take a test at school, the room is very quiet. Try to duplicate that feeling at home. Sit in a chair at a desk or table, just as you would in school.

- Finish one test at a time. Do not try to finish all of the tests in this book in one session. It is better to complete just one activity at a time. You will learn more if you stop at the end of a practice test to think about the completed questions.

- Ask questions. Talk with a family member or a friend if you find a question you do not understand. These practice tests give you the chance to check your own answers.

Look for the Test Tips throughout this workbook. They provide hints and ideas to help you find the best answers.

How to Be Test Smart

A test-smart student knows what to do when it is test-taking time. You might not know all the answers, but you will feel relaxed and focused when you take tests. Your test scores will be accurate. They will provide a snapshot of what you have learned during the school year. Here is how you can become test-smart!

Things You Can Do All Year

The best way to get ready for tests is to pay attention in school and keep up with all of your assignments. Your school curriculum is designed to teach important information and skills. However, learning does not have to stop in the classroom. Here are some ways you can become a year-round learner.

- Do your schoolwork. Standardized tests measure how much you have learned. If you keep up with your schoolwork, your test scores will reflect all the things you have learned.

- Practice smart study habits. Most people study best when they work in a quiet, clean area. Keep your study area neat. Make sure you have a calculator, dictionary, paper, and pencils nearby.

- Read a wide variety of materials, including all sorts of fiction and nonfiction. Your school or local librarian can suggest books you might not have considered reading. Read newspapers and magazines to find out about current events.

- Be a critical reader. Evaluate the quality and accuracy of everything you read. Remember that information on the Internet and in other media sources may or may not be true. It is up to you to decide which sources you can trust.

- Practice. This book is a great start to help you get ready for test day. It provides practice for all the important skills on the tests.

How to Do Your Best on Test Day

Your teacher will announce a standardized test day in advance. Follow these tips to help you succeed on the big day.

- Plan a quiet night before a test. Trying to study or memorize facts at this point might make you nervous. Enjoy a relaxing evening instead.

- Go to bed on time. You need to be well rested before the test.

- Eat a balanced breakfast. Your body needs fuel to keep your energy high during a test. Eat foods that provide long-term energy, like eggs, yogurt, or fruit. Skip the sugary cereals—the energy they give does not last very long.

- Wear comfortable clothes. Choose an outfit that makes you feel relaxed.

- Do not worry about the other students or your friends. Everyone works at different speeds. Pay attention to answering the questions in a steady fashion. It does not matter when someone else finishes the test.

- Relax. Take a few deep breaths to help you relax. Hold your pencil comfortably and do not squeeze it. Take a break every so often to wiggle your fingers and stretch your hand.

Here are some hints and strategies to help you feel comfortable with any test. Remember these ideas while taking the tests in this book.

READ THE DIRECTIONS

This sounds obvious, but every year students lose points because they assume they know the right thing to do—and they are wrong! Make sure you read and understand the directions for every test. Never assume you know what to do. Always begin by reading the directions. They will focus your attention on finding the right answers.

READ THE ANSWERS

Read the answers—ALL the answers—for a multiple-choice question, even if you think the first one is correct. Test writers sometimes put trick answers in the first or second options. You can avoid falling for this trap by reading every answer every time.

PREVIEW THE QUESTIONS

Scan each section. This will give you information about the questions. You also can see how many questions there are in the section. Do not spend too much time doing this. A quick glance will provide helpful information without making you nervous.

USE YOUR TIME WISELY

Always follow test rules. On most standardized tests, you can work on only one section at a time. Don't skip ahead or return to another section. If you finish early, go back and check your answers in that section.

- Before the test begins, find out if you can write in the test booklet. If so, add a small circle or star next to those questions that you find difficult. If time allows, come back to these questions before time is up for that section.

- Try not to spend too much time on one question. Skip a difficult question and try to answer it later. Be careful, though! You need to skip that question's number on your answer sheet. When you answer the next question, make sure you carefully fill in or darken the circle for the correct question.

- When finishing a section, look at your answer sheet. Did you answer every question for the section? Erase any extra marks on your answer sheet. Make sure you did not mark two answers for one question.

- Set your own schedule for writing exams. If you have 45 minutes to write an essay, you might decide to spend 10 minutes prewriting, 25 minutes drafting your essay, and 10 minutes revising and proofreading it.

THINK BEFORE YOU SWITCH

When you check your answers, you might be tempted to change one or more of them. In most cases, your first answer is probably the best choice. Ask yourself why you want to make a change. If you have a good reason, go ahead and pick a new answer. For example, you might have misread the question. If you cannot think of a specific reason, it is probably best to stick with your original answer choice.

MAKE AN EDUCATED GUESS

Most standardized tests take away points for wrong answers. It might be wise to skip a question if you have no idea about the answer. Leave the answer blank and move on to the next question. But if you can eliminate one or more of the answers, guessing can be a great strategy. In other words, random guessing will not help, but smart guessing can improve your test scores.

- Read every answer choice.
- Eliminate as many answers as possible.
- Try rereading or restating the question to find the best answer.
- If you decide to skip a question, make sure you leave the answer space for that question blank and move on to the next space when recording the answer for the next question.

FILL IN THE BLANKS

Many tests include fill-in-the-blank questions. The blank is usually in the middle or at the end of a sentence. Use these steps to answer a fill-in-the-blank question.

- Begin with the first answer choice. Read the sentence with that word or group of words in place of the blank. Ask yourself, "Does this answer make sense?"
- Then try filling in the blank with each of the other answer choices. Also, use the other words in the sentence as clues to help you decide the correct choice.
- Choose the best answer.

LOOK FOR CLUE WORDS

When you read test questions, watch for *clue words* that provide important information. Here are some words that make a difference.

- NOT: Many questions ask you to find the answer that is not true. These questions can be tricky. Slow down and think about the meaning of the question. Then pick the one answer that is not true.
- ALWAYS, NEVER, ALL, NONE, ONLY: These words limit a statement. They often make a generally true statement into a false one.
- SOMETIMES, SOME, MOST, MANY, OFTEN, GENERALLY: These words make a statement more believable. You will find them in many correct answers.
- BEST, MOST LIKELY, SAME, OPPOSITE, PROBABLY: These words change the meaning of a sentence. You often can use them to eliminate choices.

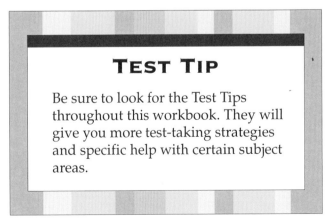

TEST TIP

Be sure to look for the Test Tips throughout this workbook. They will give you more test-taking strategies and specific help with certain subject areas.

SIX READING SKILLS

SKILL 1: DETERMINING WORD MEANINGS

Directions: Read each passage carefully. Darken the circle for the correct answer, or write your answer in the space provided.

A word can have different meanings depending on when and how you use it. Readers can figure out the correct meaning of a word by reading the sentences around it.

Don was a <u>base</u> person. He kicked dogs and used bad language.

1   In this passage, <u>base</u> means —

    A moral.

    B heavy set.

    C solid.

    D having no decency.

Hint: The second sentence explains the kind of person Don was.

He made sure the <u>base</u> of the microscope was on a level surface. He didn't want anything sliding off.

2   In this passage, the word <u>base</u> means —

    F the bottom.

    G the essential ingredient.

    H a center of operations.

    J a substance that forms a salt.

Hint: In this context, the base is part of the microscope.

I was stopped by a police officer on April 1. Unfortunately, I was informed that my registration was <u>invalid</u>. The expiration date on it was March 31.

3   In this passage, the word <u>invalid</u> means —

    A too worn to read.

    B issued to the wrong person.

    C not valid.

    D sick.

Hint: The explanation for <u>invalid</u> follows the use of the word.

He had been in the nursing home only a short time, and he had to share a room with a much older man who was in very ill health. He complained to his daughter that he was not an <u>invalid</u>. He was a fully capable person.

4   In this passage, an <u>invalid</u> means —

    F a weak, sickly person.

    G a good roommate.

    H a good father.

    J someone who is not valid.

Hint: Read the whole passage to get a sense of the word's meaning.

GO ON

Answers

1 Ⓐ Ⓑ Ⓒ ●   2 Ⓕ ● Ⓗ Ⓙ   3 Ⓐ Ⓑ ● Ⓓ   4 Ⓕ Ⓖ ● Ⓙ

Prefixes and suffixes are parts of some words. A *prefix* appears at the beginning of a word. A *suffix* appears at the end of a word. Both prefixes and suffixes affect the meaning of the word. Readers can use them to help figure out the meaning of a word.

John was a science fiction fan. He could not find enough to read about <u>extraterrestrials</u>.

1 **In this passage, the word <u>extraterrestrials</u> means —**

    A beings existing outside the earth's limits.

    B spaceships.

    C a type of terrapin.

    D the terrain on other planets.

Hint: The prefix "extra-" means beyond, or out of.

They had been to the amusement park before. Most of the rides were the same, but there was a fantastic new addition that the entire family could enjoy — a <u>monorail</u>!

2 **In this paragraph, the word <u>monorail</u> means —**

    F a type of mongoose.

    G a model railroad.

    H a single rail.

    J a one-man band.

Hint: The prefix "mono-" means one.

When he got rid of the computer, desk, easy chair, and bookcase, Joe's bedroom looked much more <u>spacious</u>.

3 **What does the word <u>spacious</u> mean in this sentence?**

clean

_____

_____

_____

_____

_____

_____

Hint: The suffix "-ious" means characterized by.

TEST TIP

Some vocabulary questions give you context clues. When you are asked to find the meaning of a vocabulary word in a passage, you will usually find at least one clear clue about the word's meaning. These items test your ability to use reasoning and find the best answer. The writers do not expect you to know the word's meaning. Take time to read the surrounding sentences and think about what they tell about the italicized or underlined word.

GO ON ➡

Answers
1 Ⓐ Ⓑ Ⓒ ●   **2** Ⓕ Ⓖ ● Ⓙ

Sometimes you can figure out the meaning of a new or difficult word by using words around it as clues.

Garbage has always been a problem in big towns. In the 1700s, Benjamin Franklin had an idea for a municipal program in Philadelphia. He wanted to hire workers to dump garbage into the river.

1   **In this paragraph, the word municipal means —**

A   hungry.

B   country.

C   real.

D   city.

Hint: Read sentences 1 and 2.

A trademark is the right a company has to own a brand name. No one else can use a trademark without the permission of the company that is the proprietor.

2   **In this paragraph, the word proprietor means —**

F   company name.

G   writer.

H   owner.

J   same brand.

Hint: Replace the underlined word with each of the choices.

One popular misconception is that the Romans used two-wheeled chariots in battle. Although they raced with these small horse-drawn vehicles, they never fought with them.

3   **What does the word chariots mean in this paragraph?**

Vehicles that were drawn by horses

Hint: The underlined word is described in the passage.

Answers

1   Ⓐ Ⓑ Ⓒ ⬤   2   Ⓕ Ⓖ ⬤ Ⓙ

Specialized or technical words are words used in specific subjects, such as science and social studies. Readers can use all the other information in the text to help determine the meaning of these words.

Mark Twain went bankrupt after buying a machine for printing. After he lost his money, he paid off his debts by lecturing. He hated to lecture.

1 In this paragraph, the word bankrupt means —

A unable to work.

B home.

C unable to pay debts.

D into business.

Hint: Read the first two sentences.

Some Native American tribes were nomads. They moved from place to place following the buffalo, which were their food supply.

2 In this paragraph, the word nomads means —

F wanderers.

G settlers.

H voters.

J builders.

Hint: Find the choice that describes people who move from place to place.

Many people believe that Rome is the oldest metropolis still in existence. But other cities are much older. Rome was founded in 753 B.C. Damascus, Syria, was founded in 3000 B.C.

3 How is the word metropolis used in this paragraph?

City state

Hint: Think about what the paragraph is all about. What is the main idea?

TEST TIP

Technical words have special meanings in some subject areas. For example, you might have a lot of *work* every day, but in science, the word *work* describes the energy used when a force moves an object. When you read a science or social studies passage, watch for unusual meanings of familiar words.

Answers

1 Ⓐ Ⓑ Ⓒ Ⓓ   2 Ⓕ Ⓖ Ⓗ Ⓙ

Some facts or details are important. By noticing and remembering them, you will better understand what the passage is about.

When he was a child, Ray Ewry became ill with a fever. His doctors told him that he had polio. Polio is a disease that causes people to become paralyzed. Ray gradually got better, but he found that his legs had been weakened by his illness. The doctors thought that leg exercises might help him regain his strength. But they told Ray that he probably would never be able to walk and run as he once had.

For the next few years, Ray exercised daily. He did everything his doctors had recommended and more. After a while he could tell that his hard work was paying off. His legs became stronger and stronger. He even began to take part in track and field events.

1 **The disease that Ray Ewry had was —**

A the measles.

B chicken pox.

C polio.

D tuberculosis.

Hint: Read the paragraph that talks about the disease.

2 **When he got better, Ray found that his legs were —**

F stronger.

G weaker.

H longer than before he got sick.

J broken.

Hint: Read the section about Ray getting better.

3 **For the next few years, Ray exercised —**

A every two weeks.

B once a month.

C weekly.

D daily.

Hint: Look for the sentence that starts with the same words.

4 **How did Ray overcome his disease?**

Ray exercised daily

Hint: Read the last paragraph.

TEST TIP

When you have to provide a short answer, begin by restating the question. This strategy will make sure that your answer stays on target. For example, to answer question 3, begin by writing, "Ray overcame his disease by . . ."

GO ON ➡

Answers

1 Ⓐ Ⓑ ● Ⓓ   2 Ⓕ ● Ⓗ Ⓙ   3 Ⓐ Ⓑ Ⓒ ●

Soon Ray could jump higher and farther than most people. So he entered the Olympics in 1900 and signed up for three contests. He entered the standing high jump; the standing long jump; and the standing hop, step, and jump. He won gold medals, or first place, in all three events.

Ray repeated his amazing feat in 1904 and planned to try again in 1906. But before the next games, the hop, step, and jump was dropped from the list of events. So Ray had to settle for only two gold medals in 1906 and two again in 1908. Ray had indeed overcome his illness. Today, he holds the record for the most Olympic gold medals ever given to any one person.

5 **In the 1900 Olympics, Ray entered —**

    A two events.

    B three events.

    C one event.

    D four events.

Hint: Find the section that describes the events Ray entered in 1900.

6 **In 1900, Ray won gold medals in —**

    F one event.

    G two events.

    H three events.

    J four events.

Hint: Read the section about the 1900 Olympics.

7 **Ray holds the record for the most —**

    A jumps.

    B events.

    C gold medals.

    D Olympics.

Hint: Read the last sentence in the second paragraph.

8 **Why was Ray unable to win the same gold medals in 1906 that he had won in 1904?**

_____

_____

_____

_____

_____

_____

_____

_____

Hint: Read how the games changed in 1906.

TEST TIP

When a question begins with *why*, look for a cause-and-effect relationship. Find information in the passage that gives exactly the reason *why* something happened. Look for the most logical reason.

Restate a *why* question using *because*. For example, begin your answer to question 8 by writing "Ron was unable to win the same medals because . . ."

GO ON

Answers

5 Ⓐ ● Ⓒ Ⓓ   **6** Ⓕ Ⓖ ● Ⓙ   **7** Ⓐ Ⓑ ● Ⓓ

Sometimes it is helpful to arrange events in the order they happened. This may help you to understand the passage better.

Boomerangs are one of the world's oldest weapons. They have been around for thousands of years. Scientists claim to have found a boomerang more than 2,400 years old, which makes the boomerang older than the bow and arrow.

The boomerang is usually thought of in connection with Australia, but it was used for hunting in Asia, Europe, and Africa, too. It was the Australian Aborigines, however, who designed boomerangs that returned after being thrown.

James Cook was the first explorer to see the Australian boomerang. In 1770, he described the strange flying sticks. The name probably came from a word that meant "wind." No one knows how the returning boomerang was invented. But scientists guess that a hunter accidentally made a curved throwing stick that came back.

Boomerangs are curved like a plane's wings on the top. They are flat on the bottom. This design helps them lift in the wind. Scientist T. L. Mitchell was the first person to explain why a boomerang returns. He wrote a paper about it in 1842.

1 When did James Cook first see boomerangs?

A when he went hunting

B before Mitchell studied boomerangs

C thousands of years ago

D when he went to Asia

Hint: Compare each of the choices to when James Cook saw boomerangs.

2 When were boomerangs invented?

F before James Cook traveled to Australia

G millions of years ago

H after the bow and arrow

J in 1842

Hint: Compare each of the choices to the invention of the boomerang.

3 What happened first?

A Captain Cook saw boomerangs.

B The Australian Aborigines used boomerangs.

C T.L. Mitchell wrote a paper on boomerangs.

D The bow and arrow was invented.

Hint: You need to read all four paragraphs.

4 Why are boomerangs able to lift in the wind?

_____

_____

_____

_____

_____

_____

_____

Hint: Read the last paragraph.

TEST TIP

Pay close attention to words that tell time order, such as *next, then, last, when, before, during,* and *after.*

GO ON ➡

Answers

1 Ⓐ Ⓑ Ⓒ Ⓓ   2 Ⓕ Ⓖ Ⓗ Ⓙ   3 Ⓐ Ⓑ Ⓒ Ⓓ

Written instructions tell the reader how to do something. To follow them means to do them in the same order in which they were written.

Eric had to be especially careful cleaning the gutters because he was the one on the ladder and his friend was there only to hold the ladder. Eric carried a hose and a gardening tool up the ladder with him. The tool had a long handle; with it he was able to reach up and remove the leaves from the gutter above him. Once all the leaves were out, Eric ran the hose into the gutter to make sure it was running freely. He also sprayed the roof. Then he descended to the ground.

1   **Eric ran the hose in the gutter —**

     A   before his friend held the ladder.

     B   after he cleaned out the gutter.

     C   after he sprayed the roof.

     D   after he climbed down the ladder.

Hint: Write down the sequence of events.

2   **According to the passage, what was the first thing Eric did?**

     F   carry the hose up the ladder

     G   clean out the gutters

     H   put up the ladder

     J   treated his friend to breakfast as a way of saying thanks

Hint: Usually, the first step is mentioned at the start.

The model looked simple enough to assemble. Referring to the instructions, Nick first made sure that he had all the pieces required. He glued the chassis together, affixing the decals as he went along. The wheels simply snapped into place. After putting the batteries into both the remote and the car, he was ready to take it for a test drive.

3   **Nick put the wheels on —**

     A   before referring to the instructions.

     B   before inserting the batteries.

     C   before gluing the chassis together.

     D   before gathering all necessary pieces.

Hint: Read the entire paragraph.

4   **What did Nick do before he began assembling the model?**

_____

_____

_____

_____

_____

_____

_____

Hint: Read the beginning of the paragraph.

STOP

Answers

1 Ⓐ Ⓑ Ⓒ Ⓓ   2 Ⓕ Ⓖ Ⓗ Ⓙ   3 Ⓐ Ⓑ Ⓒ Ⓓ

SKILL 3: SUMMARIZING MAIN IDEAS

The main idea is the overall meaning of a piece of writing. Often the main idea is written in the passage.

The harmless hognose snake is a champion bluffer. When this snake is threatened, it hisses and acts as if it will bite. If you don't run away, the hognose snake plays dead. It rolls over on its back, wiggling around as if it's in distress. Then it "dies" with its mouth open and tongue hanging out. If you turn it on its stomach, the snake will roll over on its back again.

1   The story mainly tells —

A   where the hognose snake is found.

B   what things frighten the hognose snake.

C   how dangerous the hognose snake is.

D   how the hognose snake bluffs.

Hint: The main idea is mentioned at the beginning of the passage.

Doctors think that wearing red-tinted glasses can relieve sadness. Some people get very moody and sad in the winter. They may be affected by the short days. Bright lights can help some people, but not everyone. The reddish light coming through rose-colored glasses seems to make people feel happy.

2   What is the main idea of this selection?

F   why happy people wear rose-colored glasses

G   why some people get sad

H   how short the daylight is in winter

J   how colored glasses may help people feel better

Hint: Again, the main idea is mentioned at the beginning.

The Marines had a problem in World War II. Orders were sent in code, but the enemy kept learning the code. Nothing could be kept secret. Then someone thought that Navajo soldiers could help the Marines. Since very few other people could speak Navajo, this language was used as a code. No one on the enemy side knew Navajo, so the messages remained a secret.

3   What does this story mainly talk about?

_____

_____

_____

_____

_____

_____

_____

_____

Hint: The main idea is mentioned in the passage.

TEST TIP

When you look for a *main idea*, try to find a statement that tells about the entire passage, not just one detail. The best answer makes a generalization that applies to the whole passage. Rule out answers that are too vague, too specific, or contradicted by what you just read.

GO ON

Answers
1 Ⓐ Ⓑ ● Ⓓ   2 ● Ⓖ Ⓗ Ⓙ

Skill 3: Summarizing Main Ideas

Often the main idea is not given in the text. Sometimes the reader needs to figure it out by putting the facts together.

It takes more than food for babies to grow up healthy and happy. If babies are not patted and hugged, they grow more slowly and are less healthy. Also, they will not be as smart or happy as adults who were showered with affection when they were young.

1   **The main idea of the passage is —**

A   why good food is important to babies.

B   what makes babies grow up.

C   that children need love to grow up healthy and happy.

D   how to have smart children.

Hint: What is the passage suggesting?

Probably the best-known rodeo cowboy in the world is Larry Mahan. Mahan was the national champion six times before he was thirty. He was good at every event. He was so successful that he had his own plane. When he got too old to ride, he started a rodeo school.

2   **The story mainly tells —**

F   where to ride bulls and rope calves.

G   about the most famous rodeo cowboy in the world.

H   how to get rich in the rodeo.

J   where to go to rodeo school.

Hint: You need to read the entire paragraph.

Dogs have been called our best friends, but they are also good helpers. They can be used in many ways. Some dogs hunt, while others guard animals and property. Boxers and German shepherds can be trained to lead blind people. Doctors test some medicine on dogs. A dog named Laika was the first animal in space.

3   **What is the main idea implied in the passage?**

_____

_____

_____

_____

_____

_____

_____

_____

Hint: The passage talks about dogs in general.

GO ON

Answers
1   Ⓐ Ⓑ ⬤ Ⓓ   2   Ⓕ ⬤ Ⓗ Ⓙ

A good summary contains the main idea of a passage. A good summary is brief, yet it covers the main points.

Dennis Chavez served in the United States Senate for more than twenty years. He was the first Hispanic to hold the post of senator. He was born in an adobe house in New Mexico. As a boy, he learned to speak English and taught it to his family. In 1920, he graduated from law school. Fifteen years later, he was elected senator from New Mexico. In 1991, a postage stamp with his picture was issued. The stamp honors his service to the country.

1   What is the best summary of this passage?

A Dennis Chavez was elected senator in 1935.

B Dennis Chavez was the first Hispanic United States senator.

C Dennis Chavez taught his family to speak English.

D Dennis Chavez worked at the post office.

Hint: Look for the statement that sums up the passage.

Many people take aspirin for aches and pains. Aspirin was first sold around 1900 by the Bayer Company of Germany. It was sold under the trademark "Aspirin." Then World War I swept across the world, and Germany lost the war. Under its terms of surrender, Germany agreed to release the trademark. The name Aspirin could no longer be used to sell only Bayer's product. It became the common name of a drug that can get rid of pain.

2   Write a brief summary of this passage.

_____

_____

_____

_____

_____

_____

_____

Hint: Be sure to include the main idea of the passage.

TEST TIP

When you are writing a summary for a test, include only the most important ideas. Use clear language to tell about the passage. Leave out specific or irrelevant details.

GO ON

Answers
1 Ⓐ ● Ⓒ Ⓓ

Most slaves did not become famous, but Aesop was unusual. He was a clever, witty Greek slave who earned his freedom through his cleverness. He used his animal fables for the purpose of teaching people to respect the rights of others. Two thousand years later, people continue to use his stories to teach lessons or gain helpful advice.

3 **Which of the following is the best summary of this passage?**

    F Some Greeks were slaves.

    G Aesop's fables are still used to teach important lessons.

    H People have finally learned to respect others.

    J Many slaves became famous after they were freed.

Hint: Look for the statement that sums up the passage.

The akita is a Japanese hunting dog with short, bristly hair. It is considered a symbol of good health. In fact, the dog is so prized that it has been made an official national treasure of Japan. The first akita was brought into this country in 1937. Its owner was Helen Keller, the blind and deaf author.

4 **What is this passage mostly about?**

    A Japan's national treasures

    B Akitas were brought to the United States in 1937.

    C the fame of the akitas

    D Akitas are very popular in the United States.

Hint: Which choice best describes the passage as a whole?

Acrophobia means "fear of heights." People who have this fear are known as *acrophobics*. They aren't any less afraid even when there are fences or railings to protect them. Their fear is not just one of falling. Acrophobics may fear the desire to jump from any height.

5 **Write a brief summary of this passage.**

_____

_____

_____

_____

_____

_____

_____

Hint: Write about the main point of the passage.

STOP

Answers

3 Ⓕ Ⓖ Ⓗ Ⓙ   **4** Ⓐ Ⓑ Ⓒ Ⓓ

Often when we read, we need to see cause-and-effect relationships. Knowing what happened and what made it happen will help us to understand what we read better.

You may have seen movies in which the Roman emperor shows that a gladiator should die by turning down his thumb. Actually, the gory Roman custom was to turn a thumb up toward the heart to indicate death. A thumb down meant that the soldier should be allowed to live.

1   You can tell from the passage that death probably occurred —

   A   once out of every five times.

   B   when the emperor gave a thumbs up.

   C   when the emperor gave a thumbs down.

   D   only in the movies and not in real-life Rome.

Hint: Death is the effect. What is the cause?

In New York's Federal Reserve Bank, workers handle money and other valuable metals. One of the heaviest things workers must carry is a gold brick. For this reason, some of them wear special shoes made of magnesium. These shoes protect workers' toes if a brick falls on them.

2   Workers wear special shoes because —

   F   they handle money.

   G   they work in a bank.

   H   they carry a gold brick.

   J   they have special toes.

Hint: The special shoes are the effect. Why are they worn?

The anableps is a freshwater fish found in Mexico and parts of South America. It is unusual because of its eyes. A band of skin divides each eye in half, giving it four eyes. It stays near the top of the water. It can look above and below the water at the same time.

3   What is the best reason for why the anableps might have four eyes?

   A   so it can live in Mexico

   B   so it can see better than other fish

   C   so it can live near the top of the water

   D   There is no reason.

Hint: The four eyes are the cause. What happens as a result of having them?

Today's typewriter keyboard was first designed to slow down the speed of typing. The first typists typed too fast. This made the typewriters jam. The keys were arranged as they are today in order to force typists to slow down.

4   According to the passage, what made typists slow down?

_____

_____

_____

_____

_____

_____

_____

Hint: Slowing down is the effect. What made this happen?

GO ON

Answers

1 Ⓐ Ⓑ Ⓒ ●   2 ● Ⓖ Ⓗ Ⓙ   3 Ⓐ ● Ⓒ Ⓓ

Often the reader can predict or tell in advance, what is probably going to happen next. The reader must think about what would make sense if the story were to continue.

Kay threw her bike down wherever she stopped. More than once, she had left her bicycle in the driveway. Several times her dad had pointed out what could happen when she did this. One morning, as her dad was leaving for work, Kay heard a crashing sound outside.

1   **What will Kay probably do next?**

   A   walk to school

   B   buy a new bicycle

   C   run outside

   D   put her bicycle away

   Hint: Based on the other sentences, what seems most likely to happen next?

Charlotte admired her mother's pearl ring. One morning, she decided she would wear it without her mother's permission. She dropped it in her purse and decided she would put it on at school. Later, she remembered the ring. When she reached into her purse, it was not there.

2   **What is Charlotte likely to do next?**

   F   go through the contents of her purse more carefully

   G   dump her purse out in the hall

   H   call her mother

   J   go to her next class

   Hint: Think about what you might do if you were Charlotte.

Mary worked as a cook in a cafe. One day she got the great idea to cook the world's largest pancake. For days she worked to build a giant frying pan. Then, she mixed pancake batter all night long. Next, she poured the batter into the pan and heard the familiar sizzle.

3   **What might happen next?**

   A   Mary will go to work in the cafe.

   B   Mary will become famous.

   C   Mary will have to prove that her pancake is the world's largest.

   D   The pancake will burn.

   Hint: Read the entire paragraph to determine what Mary is most likely to do.

Polio was once one of the most dreaded diseases in the United States. But in 1955, Jonas E. Salk helped change that. His polio vaccine was given to thousands of schoolchildren in Pittsburgh, Pennsylvania. Not one of the children came down with a case of polio.

4   **What do you think happened next?**

_____

_____

_____

_____

_____

_____

   Hint: Think about who else might benefit from this vaccine?

STOP

Answers

1 (A) (B) (C) (D)   2 (F) (G) (H) (J)   3 (A) (B) (C) (D)

Often texts come with graphs or diagrams. These are there to help the reader understand the passage better.

Brazil's Racial Mix in 1989

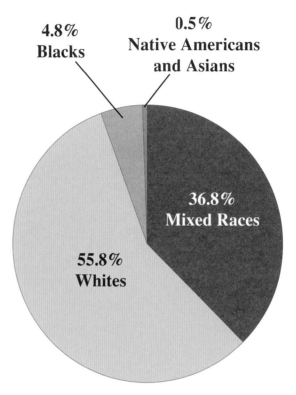

When the Portuguese arrived in Brazil early in the 16th century, it is estimated that there were between one and two million Native American people. They were used as slaves, and many thousands died from diseases brought by the Europeans. Upon arrival in Brazil, the Portuguese settlers developed vast sugarcane estates, and for 150 years these estates were the world's main source of sugar. To work the estates, the owners used slaves from Africa. During Brazil's 400 years of Portuguese rule, marriages between Europeans and Native Americans, and Europeans and Africans, produced two new groups: the olive-skinned mestizos and the darker mulattos.

1 **Which was the largest ethnic group in Brazil in 1989?**

   A Native Americans

   B Portuguese

   C whites

   D those of mixed races

   Hint: Look at the graph.

2 **How did the arrival of the Portuguese change Brazil's population?**

   _____

   _____

   _____

   _____

   Hint: Read the passage and review the chart.

GO ON ➡

Answers
1 Ⓐ Ⓑ ⒸⒹ

WIND-CHILL FACTORS — EQUIVALENT TEMPERATURES

Air Temperature (°F)

Wind Speed (mph)	35	30	25	20	15	10	5	0	−5
0	35	30	25	20	15	10	5	0	5
5	33	27	21	16	12	6	0	−5	−10
10	22	16	10	4	−3	−9	−15	−24	−27
15	16	9	2	−5	−11	−18	−25	−32	−38
20	12	4	−3	−10	−17	−25	−31	−39	−46
25	5	0	−7	−15	−22	−29	−36	−44	−51
30	0	−2	−10	−18	−25	−33	−41	−48	−56

SHADED AREA
Danger from freezing of exposed flesh

Wind is the movement of air across the earth's surface. It has an important effect on the weather. For instance, when cold air meets warm air, clouds and precipitation often form. Wind is caused by the heating of the atmosphere by the sun. Air that is warmed by the sun rises. This creates a kind of vacuum that is filled by cooler air. The movement of the air is wind.

Wind direction is measured by a weather vane or windsock. Wind speed can be measured by an instrument called an anemometer. It can also be measured by observation. The Beaufort scale is used when measuring wind by eye. It is numbered from 1 to 12. Another kind of measurement, called the wind-chill factor, involves the relationship between wind speed and temperature. The wind-chill factor is an indication of how much colder the wind makes the air feel.

3 **What makes you feel coldest?**

F a temperature of 5 degrees and a wind of 5 miles per hour

G a temperature of 15 degrees and a wind of 15 miles per hour

H a temperature of 10 degrees and a wind of 10 miles per hour

J a temperature of 30 degrees and a wind of 30 miles per hour

Hint: You need to read the chart to determine the answer.

4 **Why might it be important to know the wind-chill factor?**

A If the wind-chill factor is 35 degrees, you know there's no wind.

B If the wind-chill factor is -25 degrees or below, you could get frostbite.

C Knowing the wind-chill factor will help you measure wind speed.

D If you know the wind-chill factor, you can predict the next day's weather.

Hint: Compare the choices to the chart.

TEST TIP

Before a test begins, find out if you are allowed to mark the test booklet. If you can, underlining or circling data in tables can help you compare answers. For example, to answer question 3, circle the equivalent temperature for each temperature/wind combination in the answer choices.

GO ON

Answers
3 Ⓕ Ⓖ Ⓗ ⬤   4 ⬤ Ⓑ Ⓒ Ⓓ

Skill 5: Making Inferences and Generalizations

When a reader makes an inference, it means that the information in the passage has told the reader something indirectly.

Mosquitoes are a tremendous problem in the summer. Mosquitoes love the hot weather. Then they can fly around and bite as many people as they want. Mosquitoes can't beat their wings in cool weather. The temperature must be more than sixty degrees for mosquitoes to fly.

1 **You may conclude after reading the passage that —**

  A   mosquitoes die in cold weather.

  B   people are not bothered by mosquitoes.

  C   mosquitoes go south for the winter.

  D   cool weather means fewer mosquito bites.

  Hint: Although never stated, the passage implies something.

When Jim Abbott was born, part of his right arm had not formed completely. He had only one working hand, but Jim made the most of his situation. In college, Jim became the star pitcher of the baseball team. He played so well that he was later signed by a professional team. Jim Abbott became a major league player.

2 **What does this passage infer?**

  F   Abbott overcame his disability.

  G   People were not impressed by Abbott's skill.

  H   In college, Abbott was lazy.

  J   Abbott always regretted his disability.

  Hint: Look for the choice that is not written in the passage, but implied.

One day, as Janna was jogging, she spotted something in the grass, so she decided to investigate. It was a wallet full of money. Janna knew she could keep the money, and no one would ever find out. But Janna also knew that the person who lost the wallet probably needed the money. So, she took the wallet to the police.

3 **What can you conclude about Janna's personality after reading this passage?**

  _____

  _____

  _____

  _____

  _____

  _____

  _____

  Hint: Janna's actions in the story tell you something about her.

GO ON

Answers
  1 Ⓐ Ⓑ Ⓒ ⬤   2 Ⓕ ⬤ Ⓗ Ⓙ

SKILL 5: MAKING INFERENCES AND GENERALIZATIONS

Sometimes a reader needs to generalize. This means to come up with a general statement about something in the text.

In 1883, a California mailman named Jim Stacy found a stray dog that he named Dorsey. Dorsey accompanied Stacy on his mail route. But later, Stacy got sick. So he tied the mail along with a note to Dorsey's back and sent the dog out alone. Dorsey delivered the mail in this fashion until 1886.

1 **From this paragraph you can guess that —**

   A Stacy was sick for a long time.

   B Dorsey would never leave Stacy's side.

   C the note told people what to feed Dorsey.

   D Dorsey received a medal from the post office.

Hint: Generalize what might have happened.

The parasol ant of South America gets its name from the way it carries a bit of leaf over its head. But native Brazilians call them doctor ants. They use the ants' strong jaws to clamp down on deep cuts and keep them closed. Once the jaws clamp, the Brazilians pinch off the ants' bodies to keep the wound sealed.

2 **From the passage, you can make the general statement that —**

   F parasol ants haven't been named correctly.

   G the ants' jaws stay closed after the ants die.

   H native Brazilians named the ants "parasol ants."

   J the ants like sunshine.

Hint: Which choice is the best guess?

Great Britain may not be the place where golf was first played. The ancient Romans played a similar game. They used a curved stick and a leather ball stuffed with feathers. The Romans occupied Great Britain until A.D. 400.

3 **From this story, you could make the generalization that golf —**

   A began in A.D. 400.

   B began in Great Britain and moved to Rome.

   C began in Rome and moved to Great Britain.

   D is played more today in Rome than in Great Britain.

Hint: Eliminate the choices that can be proved untrue.

GO ON ➡

Answers
1 Ⓐ Ⓑ Ⓒ ⬤   **2** ⬤ Ⓖ Ⓗ Ⓙ   **3** Ⓐ Ⓑ ⬤ Ⓓ

A good reader will analyze what he or she reads and make his or her own judgment about the text. Often things are implied in a text, rather than stated directly.

People around the world eat many different things. Some people eat worms and ants. In some areas of the world, termites are considered a healthy food. They make delicious, bite-sized snacks. They are even served with hamburgers.

1   What judgment can you make after reading this paragraph?

   A   Eating habits differ around the world.

   B   Hamburgers are made of ants and worms.

   C   Everyone in the world eats the same things.

   D   Termites are better than worms.

Do you like peanut butter? Most people do. Naturally, peanut butter is made from peanuts. But peanuts are used in the manufacture of other things. Items such as ink dyes, shaving cream, paper, and shoe polish use peanuts in some form.

2   The passage suggests that —

   F   peanut butter is a good shaving cream.

   G   shoe polish tastes like peanut butter.

   H   it is easy to write on a peanut.

   J   peanuts are very useful.

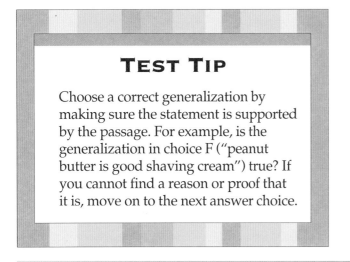

TEST TIP

Choose a correct generalization by making sure the statement is supported by the passage. For example, is the generalization in choice F ("peanut butter is good shaving cream") true? If you cannot find a reason or proof that it is, move on to the next answer choice.

The giant saguaro cactus plant is often seen in American Western movies. Although the largest plants can grow to be forty feet tall, they grow very slowly at first. The stem of the plant grows about one inch during its first ten years, but later it grows at a faster rate. The largest saguaros can live for almost two hundred years.

3   Based on the information in the passage, the saguaro would most likely be found —

   A   in Japan.

   B   in New York.

   C   in the Middle East.

   D   in Arizona.

Hint: None of the choices are stated in the passage, but one of them is a conclusion that the reader can determine after reading the text.

Elizabeth Tashjian runs the world's only nut museum. The museum is found on the first floor of an old mansion, which is also her home. Her collection of nuts from around the world is always being raided by bushy-tailed thieves that live near the house.

4   What were the bushy-tailed thieves that raided the museum?

_____

_____

_____

_____

Hint: The clues are in the passage.

GO ON

Answers
1 Ⓐ Ⓑ Ⓒ Ⓓ   2 Ⓕ Ⓖ Ⓗ Ⓙ   3 Ⓐ Ⓑ Ⓒ Ⓓ

The setting is the when and where of a story. The characters are the people or people-like figures in the story. The plot is the sequence of events that make up the core of the story.

The organ starts, and its music fills the air. The horses slowly begin to move. Riders hold tightly as their colorful horses go up and down and around and around.

1 What is the setting of this passage?

_____

_____

_____

_____

Hint: Picture the scene in your mind.

In the 17th century, the Incas of South America had an empire that stretched more than 2,500 miles. They built highways throughout their empire. They built tunnels through mountain cliffs. One of their rope suspension bridges is still used today.

2 The Incas Empire was in —

   A the southern United States.

   B South Africa.

   C South America.

   D a southern state.

Hint: Read the first sentence.

3 This passage describes a period of time in the —

   F 1600s.

   G 1700s.

   H 1800s.

   J 1900s.

Hint: Read the first sentence.

In Greek legends, Orpheus was a singer of sweet music. As a young man, he married a beautiful woman named Eurydice. But then she stepped on a poisonous snake and died. Orpheus was filled with grief, and he decided to go to the underworld to win his wife back from death. In the dark caverns below the earth, he charmed Hades, king of the underworld, with his sad song. Hades agreed to release Eurydice on one condition: Orpheus could not look back at her until they reached the earth's surface. Orpheus agreed, and he began to lead his wife from the darkness. But just once, to make sure she was still following, Orpheus looked back. His dear wife vanished instantly.

4 Which of the characters is very powerful?

   A Orpheus

   B Eurydice

   C Hades

   D none of the characters

Hint: Think about what each character did.

5 Describe the overall mood that the author establishes in this passage.

_____

_____

_____

_____

_____

_____

Hint: Think about the words used to tell the story.

STOP

Answers
2 Ⓐ Ⓑ Ⓒ Ⓓ   **3** Ⓕ Ⓖ Ⓗ Ⓙ   **4** Ⓐ Ⓑ Ⓒ Ⓓ

The author's point of view is what he or she feels about what he or she is writing. Opinions express points of view.

The island of Surtsey, off the southern coast of Iceland, was the first new island to appear in the North Atlantic in two hundred years. Scientists studied how plant life began on the island and how long the island may last. They determined whether the island would be destroyed by the same volcano that created it. Their research gave the public a wealth of information about this unusual island.

1   The author feels that the scientists' study of Surtsey —

    A made it famous.

    B made them wealthy.

    C was unnatural.

    D was a waste of their time.

Hint: Read the entire paragraph.

Would you like to come home after a long day and walk into an elephant? You would do that if you lived in The Elephant House in Margate, New Jersey, which was built in 1881 by James Lafferty. Herbert Green built a chicken-shaped house in 1962. Sarah Winchester spent 38 years building a ghost-proof house with fake chimneys, doors that opened into walls, and stairs that led nowhere. And a man named Baldasera spent forty years building an underground house with ninety rooms for about $300. If you think your plans for a house are too unusual, think again!

2   This author believes that —

    F no house plans are too unusual.

    G people should stick with traditional designs.

    H underground homes are impractical.

    J homes should be built quickly.

Hint: Think about what the author says about homes.

Bill Cosby had planned to be a teacher one day. But he dropped out of college and became a successful actor instead. In 1971, he decided to go back to school. He finished his degree and went to receive his doctor of education degree in 1977. As part of his coursework, he developed programs for *Sesame Street* and *The Electric Company*. He also worked with Captain Kangaroo to produce *Picture Page*, a television series for children.

3   The point of view this author expresses is that —

    A you should never give up on your dreams.

    B Cosby became successful because of children's programming.

    C Cosby would have been a better teacher than he was an actor.

    D it took Cosby too long to get his degree.

Hint: Review each choice. With which one would the author most likely agree?

The whole family once piled into the car and headed to the drive-in movies. Beneath the stars, we would munch popcorn and watch a movie. The first drive-in movie opened in New Jersey in 1933. Now there are only a few left.

4   What does the author think of drive-in movies?

_____

_____

_____

_____

_____

_____

Hint: What feeling do you get when you read this?

GO ON ➡

Answers

1 Ⓐ Ⓑ Ⓒ Ⓓ   2 Ⓕ Ⓖ Ⓗ Ⓙ   3 Ⓐ Ⓑ Ⓒ Ⓓ

Skill 6: Recognizing Points of View, Facts, and Opinions

Often authors want to convince their readers of something. To do this, they will write only about their own point of view. They use descriptive and emotional language that backs up their point of view.

How much is a seat in Congress worth: $5 million, $17 million, $30 million? In a recent California election, two millionaires were vying for the same Senate seat. Together they spent more than $30 million on their campaigns. The losing candidate spent more than $17 million in his bid to be senator. Isn't it time we reigned in this extravagance? We need to develop laws that stop the buying of seats in Congress. Only by limiting the amount of money candidates may receive and use when running for office will we be able to reduce the extravagance that now exists in Congressional elections.

1 **Which of the statements below is an opinion?**

    A Millionaires are running for Congress.

    B Running for Congress has become an extravagance.

    C Having $17 million does not guarantee a seat in Congress.

    D A candidate is someone who runs for office.

Hint: An opinion is a point of view.

2 **What does the author of this editorial want U.S. citizens to do?**

_____

_____

_____

_____

_____

_____

_____

Hint: Read the entire paragraph.

The President has proposed that all young Americans be encouraged to participate in a national service plan. The theory is that this will instill a greater sense of community in this so-called "lost" generation. The younger generation is supposedly selfish, but the facts don't warrant these conclusions. Over 800 colleges have organized volunteer efforts, and most high schools have students doing community service. Troubled young adults are the exception, not the rule; the press reports the opposite in its effort to sell papers. In order to teach young people the skills and values necessary to become productive citizens, it would be far better to increase the number of young people in the private sector.

3 **Which statement best expresses the author's opinion about national service programs?**

    F They are being introduced by the President.

    G They have benefited our country through the years.

    H They will rebuild the American Dream.

    J They are not as effective as the private sector in teaching values.

Hint: Read the entire paragraph.

4 **Who does the author blame for creating the public opinion that young adults are selfish?**

_____

_____

_____

_____

_____

Hint: The answer is stated in the paragraph.

GO ON ➡

Answers

   1 Ⓐ Ⓑ Ⓒ Ⓓ   **3** Ⓕ Ⓖ Ⓗ Ⓙ

SKILL 6: RECOGNIZING POINTS OF VIEW, FACTS, AND OPINIONS

It is important to recognize the difference between fact and opinion. A fact is real and true. An opinion states a point of view. Descriptive words are used to offer opinions.

Most people are afraid of something. A study was conducted to determine what people fear most. The research found that men and women tend to have the same fears. The basic difference is the order in which they rate these fears. For example, men fear bats and speaking in public more than women do. Women fear fire, dead people, and rats more than men do.

1   It is a fact that —

   A   men's and women's fears are somewhat alike and yet different.

   B   everyone likes rats.

   C   women fear bats more than men do.

   D   everyone is afraid of chickens.

   Hint: Which choice best matches what is said in the story?

Some animals can help predict earthquakes. This was proven in China in 1974. Just a few months before a huge earthquake struck an area, animals began acting strangely. Hens wouldn't roost, and geese wouldn't fly. Pigs tried climbing walls and fought with each other. Even hibernating snakes crawled out of the ground. The Chinese paid attention to these warnings. Many people left the area before the earthquake struck.

2   This passage states the fact that —

   F   some animals know if an earthquake is going to occur.

   G   many earthquakes occur in China.

   H   the pigs were fighting with the chickens.

   J   animals in China act strange all the time.

   Hint: You need to read the entire paragraph.

Man o' War was a wonderful racehorse. He won 20 of 21 races and set five world records. When Man o' War died in 1947, his owner, Samuel Riddle, had him buried. Riddle, who died in 1963, remembered the horse in his will. He left $4 million to maintain Man o' War's grave, which the horse richly deserved.

3   Which of the following is a fact?

   A   Man o' War was a wonderful racehorse.

   B   Man o' War died in 1947.

   C   Samuel Riddle was an eccentric person.

   D   The horse deserved a $4 million inheritance.

   Hint: A fact is real and true.

Sarah Winnemucca was a pioneer of Native American rights. Her father was a chief of the Paiute tribe in Nevada. As a child, she moved to California, where she lived with a white family. She learned to speak English. As an adult, she became a teacher and tried to make peace between the white settlers and her native tribe. She even met to discuss the situation with President Hayes. She gained the support of many people, and her efforts were valuable.

4   It is the writer's opinion that Winnemucca —

   F   should not have moved to California.

   G   was a good teacher.

   H   liked President Hayes.

   J   made worthwhile efforts.

   Hint: Look at the words that describe Winnemucca.

GO ON

Answers

1 (A) (B) (C) (D)   2 (F) (G) (H) (J)   3 (A) (B) (C) (D)   4 (F) (G) (H) (J)

Sometimes the point of view will change during a story. A character can change how he or she feels and/or the mood of a story can change.

Bob had two left feet. He was so embarrassed, that he would never get up and dance. One day, he decided to do something about it, so he signed up for dance lessons. The dance instructor told him how to move his feet. It was supposed to be the box step; unfortunately, Bob tripped over his own feet.

After several lessons, Bob could do the box step smoothly and with confidence. He couldn't wait to get up and dance.

1   With which statement would the author of this passage most likely agree?

A Some people should never try to dance.

B Do not give up.

C Lessons never help you to improve.

D Some people are natural born dancers.

Hint: Read the last paragraph.

2   How did Bob change during the story?

_____

_____

_____

_____

_____

_____

_____

Hint: Read the first two and last two sentences.

"I don't want to write a story about girls! I don't know anything about girls," Louisa May Alcott told her publisher, Mr. Niles. But she was desperate for money. So Louisa wrote a simple story about growing up with four sisters in a family that had no money. Her book, *Little Women*, took a year to write. Mr. Niles thought the book was dull, and so did Louisa, but in three months, all the copies of *Little Women* had sold. Mr. Niles thought he could sell three or four hundred more copies. With a great sigh of relief, Louisa was able to write to her family, "Paid off all the debts, thank the Lord! Now I feel that I could die in peace."

3   Louisa May Alcott did not want to write *Little Women* because —

F the story was too exciting for most readers.

G she hated children.

H she felt she didn't know enough about girls.

J Mr. Niles did not offer her enough money.

Hint: Read the first sentence.

4   Why was Louisa relieved after the book was published?

_____

_____

_____

_____

_____

_____

_____

Hint: Read the last 5 sentences.

Answers
1 Ⓐ ⬤ Ⓒ Ⓓ   3 Ⓕ Ⓖ ⬤ Ⓙ

READING COMPREHENSION

Directions: Read the selection carefully. Darken the circle for the correct answer, or write your answer in the space provided.

TRY THIS Read each selection and each question twice. Check your answers by looking back in the selection.

Sample A   **Cliff Dwellings**

Mesa Verde National Park, in southwestern Colorado, has some of the best examples of ancient cliff dwellings in the United States. About 800 years ago, people called the Anasazi built apartment-like dwellings in the caves of steep canyon walls.

Where is Mesa Verde National Park?

A   New Mexico

B   Utah

C   Texas

D   Colorado

THINK IT THROUGH The correct answer is <u>D</u>. The first sentence states that the park is in southwestern Colorado.

🛑 STOP

City Living

Frieda and her mother lived in an apartment in New York City. Frieda had no brothers or sisters, and there were no children living nearby. Her best friend was a woman named Maria, who lived down the hall.

Maria's most prized possessions were a cat named Javier and an album of photographs from her family in Costa Rica. When she visited Maria, Frieda liked to study the album. Men in big mustaches and women in embroidered blouses stared from the photographs. Maria would begin by talking about these long-dead relatives but would end by telling stories about the jaguars and parrots that lived in the rain forest near her family home. Frieda loved listening to these stories. She wanted to become a scientist to help save the rain forests from destruction.

One night as Frieda was doing her homework she heard sirens, and fire trucks suddenly appeared on the street below. The next thing she knew, a firefighter was pounding on their door. The top floors of the building were on fire. Frieda's mother shouted, "Grab your stereo and let's go!" Frieda had saved her money for a year to buy the stereo.

"Maria may need help!" Frieda yelled as she raced down the hall to her friend's apartment. The door was standing open. The firefighters had already helped Maria and Javier downstairs. Frieda grabbed the heavy photo album from the shelf where Maria always kept it. Frieda hurried downstairs; smoke was filling the hallways.

Frieda's mother was anxiously waiting for her on the street. She saw that her daughter had saved only Maria's photo album. "I'm sorry about your stereo," Frieda's mother said.

"That's all right," Frieda said, "I made the right choice."

GO ON

Answers
SA Ⓐ Ⓑ Ⓒ Ⓓ

1 This selection is mostly about a girl who —

A fights a fire.

B makes a difficult choice.

C buys a stereo.

D knows how to save money.

2 According to this selection, the story takes place in —

F Costa Rica.

G the country.

H a tropical rain forest.

J New York City.

3 Why did Frieda want to become a scientist?

A to find a cure for cancer

B to become rich and famous

C to have a better life for herself and her mother

D to save the rain forests from destruction

4 Maria's most prized possessions were an album of photographs and —

F a collection of postcards.

G a parrot from Brazil.

H a cat named Javier.

J a grandfather clock.

5 Why did Frieda like to visit Maria?

A to play with her cat, Javier

B to feed the parrots and jaguars

C to talk about her day at school

D to see pictures of Maria's relatives

6 In this selection, the word embroidered means —

F decorated with fancy raised designs made with thread.

G dry clean only.

H made in Costa Rica.

J smooth-textured, imported fabric.

7 When did Frieda hurry downstairs?

A when the firefighters pounded on her door

B before she saw the fire trucks

C after she grabbed Maria's album

D when she saw Maria and her cat

8 Why did Frieda grab the photo album?

F She knew it meant a lot to Maria.

G She always wanted to own it.

H She did not see anything else to save.

J Maria told her to save it.

9 Write a new title for this selection.

_____

_____

_____

_____

_____

_____

_____

GO ON

Answers

1 Ⓐ Ⓑ Ⓒ Ⓓ   3 Ⓐ Ⓑ Ⓒ Ⓓ   5 Ⓐ Ⓑ Ⓒ Ⓓ   7 Ⓐ Ⓑ Ⓒ Ⓓ

2 Ⓕ Ⓖ Ⓗ Ⓙ   4 Ⓕ Ⓖ Ⓗ Ⓙ   6 Ⓕ Ⓖ Ⓗ Ⓙ   8 Ⓕ Ⓖ Ⓗ Ⓙ

Chicago

Skyscrapers tower
along Lake Michigan
like building blocks.

They seem to lean
toward one another
as if for support.

In their glass sides we see
a reflection in primary colors
of sunset, water, and parks.

Unknowing, they take in
their surroundings and return them
to us as a dream.

10 Describe the setting for this poem.

_____

_____

_____

_____

_____

_____

_____

11 The buildings in the poem are compared to —

A sunsets.

B blocks.

C parks.

D glass.

12 This poem was probably written to describe —

F how Chicago's skyscrapers look.

G how Chicago is like a dream.

H a sunset on Lake Michigan.

J buildings that look like they are dreaming.

13 The poem compares the reflection from the skyscrapers' glass sides to —

A real life.

B a dream.

C a subconscious desire.

D an artist's inspiration.

TEST TIP

Remember to connect ideas in all parts of a poem, paragraph, or article. To answer question 13, look at the third and fourth stanzas of the poem. If you looked only at the third stanza, you might conclude that the writer was comparing the reflection to an artist's inspiration because this stanza mentions colors. However, when you continue reading, you discover that the writer continues to talk about the reflections in the fourth stanza. With a full understanding of both stanzas, you can find the poem's most important comparison.

Answers
11 Ⓐ Ⓑ Ⓒ Ⓓ   **12** Ⓕ Ⓖ Ⓗ Ⓙ   **13** Ⓐ Ⓑ Ⓒ Ⓓ

A Letter to the Editor of the Daily Tribune

Mr. Michael Cowling, Editor

Daily Tribune

Dear Mr. Cowling,

The Monroe Library has helped me a great deal in the last few months. I was having trouble reading. My teacher told us that the library has an after-school program. The people there could help kids with homework and reading. My mom signed me up. I go to the library right after school. Ms. Rose tutors me in reading for a half-hour every day. Then I do my homework.

My grades have improved. I have more time to practice and play baseball. Mom is happy because I finish my homework early. Sometimes I go back to the library in the evening for programs like cartoon workshops and storytelling.

The library also has a homework hotline. Students can call, and someone will try to answer their questions.

I never thought the library could be so much fun. I hope you will print this letter so more kids can learn about the library's great programs.

Sincerely,

Joshua Cohen

Joshua Cohen

GO ON ➡

14 Who is Michael Cowling?

    F the reading tutor at the Monroe Library

    G the author of this letter

    H the editor of the *Daily Tribune*

    J Joshua's teacher

15 When does Joshua go to the library?

    A on the weekends

    B after school

    C before school

    D during lunch

16 Who told Joshua about the after-school program?

    F his mother

    G his teacher

    H Ms. Rose

    J the librarian

17 This letter is written from the viewpoint of someone who is—

    A angry.

    B grateful.

    C confused.

    D upset.

18 Which of these is an *opinion* in the letter?

    F My grades have improved.

    G My teacher told us that the library has an after-school program.

    H I never thought the library could be so much fun.

    J Ms. Rose tutors me in reading for a half-hour every day.

19 From the letter you can conclude that Joshua—

    A will never go back to the library.

    B enjoys spending time at the library.

    C still has problems at school.

    D is not feeling well.

20 Why did Joshua go to the Monroe Library?

_____

_____

_____

_____

_____

21 This letter is written in order to—

_____

_____

_____

_____

_____

TEST TIP

Opinions on tests often contain signal words. Some words that signal an opinion are exaggerations, such as *most exciting* or *least interesting*. Other opinions name something as the *best* or *worst* or claim that one thing is *better* or *worse* than another. Opinions also use words that make judgments, such as *foolish, clever, amazing, horrible, exciting, dull,* or *fun.*

GO ON ➡

Answers

14 Ⓕ ●Ⓗ Ⓙ   **16** ●Ⓖ Ⓗ Ⓙ   **18** Ⓕ Ⓖ ● Ⓙ

15 Ⓐ Ⓑ Ⓒ ●   **17** ● Ⓑ Ⓒ Ⓓ   **19** Ⓐ Ⓑ Ⓒ Ⓓ

Niagara Falls Journal

July 24—My family and I got an early morning start on our driving vacation from Illinois to Niagara Falls in Ontario, Canada. We drove the entire 11 hours today. I am excited, because this is the first time I have visited another country. I love reading the street signs and food labels in French and English. How unusual to be in a country that is *bilingual!*

July 25—We started our day at Horseshoe Falls. Just watching all the millions of gallons of water flow over the Falls is *mesmerizing.* I couldn't take my eyes off the natural display. The noise was incredible. Where does all that water come from? My family and I decided to take the tour of the tunnels that are under Horseshoe Falls. We had to wear raincoats and ride an elevator down to the tunnels. We walked through long tunnels that made me feel *claustrophobic* until we could see daylight and hear the roar of the rushing water. Unbelievable! We were seeing the waterfall from behind. I learned the following amazing facts about the Falls: Niagara Falls is made up of two falls, the Horseshoe Falls in Canada and the American Falls in the United States. Horseshoe Falls is 167 feet (51 meters) high and 2,600 feet (792 meters) wide. American Falls is 176 feet (54 meters) high and 1,000 feet (305 meters) wide.

July 26—Today we went on the *Maid of the Mist* boat ride. Again we had to put on raincoats, but this time they were much heavier than the ones we wore in the tunnels. We needed added protection, because our boat took us past the American Falls and into the heavy mist of Horseshoe Falls. As we neared Horseshoe Falls, the noise sounded like a train coming closer and closer. It was hard to keep my balance standing in the boat, because the force of the water was so great. For a few seconds I was afraid that our boat would get swallowed by the whirlpool that the Falls create. I took some good pictures of the Falls and the rainbow produced by the mist and the sun. We came back to the Falls at night to see the light display. Hundreds of lights that constantly changed color were directed on the Falls.

July 27—We rented two tandem bicycles today. We rode the bike path along the Niagara River from Horseshoe Falls to Fort Erie. The ride was long, but the view of the rapidly moving Niagara River was gorgeous. Fort Erie was constructed by the British in 1764. It was used as a supply depot and a port for ships transporting merchandise, troops, and passengers from Lake Erie along the Niagara River to the upper Great Lakes. My favorite point of interest in the fort was the soldiers' barracks. You could see how cramped and unpleasant their daily life must have been.

July 28—We left Niagara Falls for the remainder of our trip to Toronto, Ontario. We drove along Queen Victoria Park, which parallels the Niagara River. I agree with Winston Churchill, who once remarked that this route is "the prettiest Sunday afternoon drive in the world."

GO ON ⇒

22 What is the author's mood in the first paragraph?

F nervousness

G boredom

H irritation

J enthusiasm

23 You can tell that the word *bilingual* means—

A a number system based on 2.

B having two languages.

C wealthy.

D a dry stream bed.

24 In the second journal entry, the phrase "made me feel claustrophobic" means the author was—

F afraid of water.

G willing to climb to great heights.

H afraid of confined places.

J used to traveling in boats.

25 Which is a *fact* expressed in the journal?

A I love reading the street signs and food labels in French and English.

B My favorite point of interest in the fort was the soldiers' barracks.

C American Falls is higher than Horseshoe Falls.

D The postcards sold at Niagara Falls are prettier than anywhere else on earth.

26 In the second journal entry, what word does the author use to mean "can't take my eyes off?"

F mesmerizing

G incredible

H display

J claustrophobic

27 In the third journal entry, the noise Horseshoe Falls makes is compared to—

A a boat.

B noises in tunnels.

C noise created by a whirlpool.

D that of an approaching train.

28 Why was Fort Erie built?

F as a supply depot and port

G as a place for tourists to visit

H as a lighthouse and store

J as a place for the queen to live

29 The description of the soldiers' barracks at Fort Erie helps the reader know that—

A the soldiers' families lived with them.

B the soldiers were content at the fort.

C the soldiers had many chores.

D the soldiers were very uncomfortable.

30 What does the last journal entry describe?

_____

_____

_____

_____

_____

_____

31 What was the author's purpose in keeping this journal?

_____

_____

_____

_____

_____

_____

GO ON ➡

Answers

22 Ⓕ Ⓖ Ⓗ Ⓙ   24 Ⓕ Ⓖ Ⓗ Ⓙ   26 Ⓕ Ⓖ Ⓗ Ⓙ   28 Ⓕ Ⓖ Ⓗ Ⓙ

23 Ⓐ Ⓑ Ⓒ Ⓓ   25 Ⓐ Ⓑ Ⓒ Ⓓ   27 Ⓐ Ⓑ Ⓒ Ⓓ   29 Ⓐ Ⓑ Ⓒ Ⓓ

NEW AND IMPROVED

Grade A Dog Chow

A new and improved line of dog food that combines the flavor of real beef with the essential minerals needed for a happy and healthy life
Veterinarians agree that this is the dog food to buy.

•**Essential Minerals** — Grade A Dog Chow provides your dog with 12 essential minerals for good health. This means that **Grade A Dog Chow** has three more minerals than is recommended by the National Canine Council. For example, **Grade A Dog Chow** contains zinc for healthy skin, calcium for stronger bones, and sodium for proper kidney function.

•**Real Beef** — Grade A Dog Chow contains real beef. Most dog foods are flavored with beef, but actually contain little or no real beef at all. Look at the list of ingredients on the container of your dog's food. If beef is not the first ingredient listed, then beef is not the main ingredient. We guarantee that **Grade A Dog Chow** is the only dog food on the market that lists beef first.

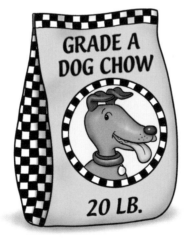

•**Disease Protection** — Grade A Dog Chow is the first and only dog food that provides your dog with protection from heartworm. Heartworm medication is in the dog food. If your dog eats the recommended amount of food each day, he or she will receive the maximum protection needed to prevent this dreaded canine disease.

•**Convenient Packaging** — Grade A Dog Chow comes in convenient one-serving size cans or in 20-pound bags.

•**Great Price** — Grade A Dog Chow is the best dog food for your money. It is a reasonable $3.69 per pound.

We guarantee your dog will not only like our dog food, but eat it with gusto, or your money back!

GO ON

32 Which of these is a *fact* in the ad?

    F Grade A Dog Chow contains real beef.

    G Grade A Dog Chow is an improved line of dog food.

    H Dogs will like Grade A Dog Chow and eat it with gusto.

    J Grade A Dog Chow is the best dog food for your money.

33 There is enough information in the ad to show that—

    A phosphorus is harmful to your dog's health.

    B no other dog food is good for your dog.

    C Grade A Dog Chow contains several minerals.

    D Grade A Dog Chow is the only dog food recommended by pet-store owners.

34 The mineral in Grade A Dog Chow that helps with proper kidney function is—

    F selenium.

    G sodium.

    H zinc.

    J calcium.

35 The ad is meant to appeal to a desire to—

    A lower the fat in the diets of dogs.

    B increase the amount of fluids retained in dogs.

    C purchase dog food from veterinarians.

    D raise a happy dog that lives a long, healthy life.

36 According to the ad, beef is the main ingredient in dog food if—

    F it is flavored with beef.

    G beef is the first ingredient listed.

    H the food contains 12 essential minerals.

    J the containers are single-serving size.

37 What does the ad claim about Grade A Dog Chow?

_____

_____

_____

_____

_____

_____

_____

TEST TIP

Question 37 does not ask you to restate every idea in the ad. Instead, it asks what general idea is *claimed* by the ad. Begin your answer by writing "The ad claims that Grade A Dog Chow . . ."

GO ON ➡

Answers

32 ● ⒢ ⒣ ⒥   **34** ● ⒢ ⒣ ⒥   **36** Ⓕ ⒢ ⒣ ●

33 Ⓐ Ⓑ Ⓒ ●   **35** Ⓐ ● Ⓒ Ⓓ

A Medical Pioneer

Today, if you need to have heart surgery, you can choose from many fine doctors. However, before 1893 this type of surgery was unknown. Doctors did not have modern medical tools and procedures essential for heart surgery, such as x-rays, antibiotics, and blood transfusions. In those days, heart patients were treated with sedatives, and they usually did not survive. Then in 1893, Daniel Hale Williams, a young African-American surgeon, attempted a new medical technique in order to save a patient's life.

One day a man named James Cornish was rushed to the emergency room in the hospital in Chicago where Dr. Williams worked. Cornish was suffering from a very serious knife wound. The knife had cut an artery less than an inch from Cornish's heart and punctured the pericardium, the sac around the heart. Dr. Williams called on six of his staff doctors to assist him with a complicated and daring operation. Dr. Williams became the first surgeon to save his patient by successfully repairing the human heart.

38 James Cornish is referred to as *patient* in the article because he—

A does not lose his temper.

B is under medical care.

C is untiring.

D does not complain about his problems.

39 Which of these would best help you understand this article?

F finding Chicago, Illinois, on a map

G looking up Daniel Hale Williams in an encyclopedia

H looking up *antibiotics* in a dictionary

J reading the history of modern medical tools

40 What happened to many heart patients before 1893?

A They were x-rayed.

B They died.

C They had surgery.

D They recovered.

41 What is another good title for this article?

_____

_____

_____

_____

STOP

Answers
38 Ⓐ Ⓑ Ⓒ Ⓓ   39 Ⓕ Ⓖ Ⓗ Ⓙ   40 Ⓐ Ⓑ Ⓒ Ⓓ

A sample question helps you to understand the type of question you will be asked in the test that follows.

Sample A   Polar Bears

Polar bears are sometimes called ice bears or snow bears. These huge bears live in the icy lands near the North Pole. They sometimes weigh more than 1,000 pounds. Their thick, white fur and layers of fat help them stay warm in the freezing winters. Polar bears live by themselves except when a mother has cubs.

Why can polar bears live near the North Pole?

A   They build fires.

B   They huddle close together.

C   They stay in caves all winter.

D   They have thick fur and layers of fat.

For questions 1–32, carefully read each selection and the questions that follow. Then darken the circle for the correct answer.

The World Food Crisis

In some parts of the world, food shortages cause many people to starve. Somehow, the world's food crop—the amount of food produced worldwide—must be increased. In order to help this happen, scientists have begun to study little-known, edible plants. There are about 20,000 kinds of edible plants, although only about 100 of them are grown as food crops.

Amaranth and leucaena are two plants that have the potential of becoming useful food crops in the near future. Amaranth is a grain that has been eaten in Mexico for hundreds of years. It can be grown in a variety of climates and soils, has many uses, and is rich in nutrients. Amaranth tastes good and can be ground and used as flour or popped like corn. Leucaena is a tree that may become a popular food source of the future. It can also be used for making fuel. This tall tree grows very fast.

As time goes on, more plants are being discovered and rediscovered. Scientists hope these plants will help solve the world's food crisis.

1   There is enough information in this article to show that—

A   meat will not be available in the future.

B   there are probably many useful edible plants that are not used as food crops.

C   leucaena is similar to broccoli.

D   amaranth probably will not be used very much as a food source in the future.

2   All are characteristics of the amaranth plant *except*—

F   it is used for making fuel.

G   it is rich in nutrients.

H   it tastes good.

J   it can be popped like corn.

3   What is this article mainly about?

_____

_____

_____

GO ON

Answers
SA Ⓐ Ⓑ Ⓒ Ⓓ   1 Ⓐ Ⓑ Ⓒ Ⓓ   2 Ⓕ Ⓖ Ⓗ Ⓙ

A Ride in an Airship

The first time I became interested in airships was when I read about the *Hindenburg* disaster. The *Hindenburg* was one of the largest airships ever built. It was about 804 feet long, 135 feet wide, and had a volume of 7,062,100 cubic feet. The *Hindenburg* was classified as a rigid airship. This kind of airship had a hull with a framework of wood or metal that supported the outer skin. Inside the hull were several gas cells that held hydrogen gas.

The *Hindenburg* was used for passenger service. There were 97 people aboard on May 6, 1937—the day it exploded while approaching its dock in Lakehurst, New Jersey. The disaster ended the development of rigid ships.

Today, there were three of us gathered who had won a contest at a local air show. Our prize was a ride in a blimp, or nonrigid airship. I was a bit *apprehensive* about accepting my prize, but I was very curious. When the blimp came to pick us up, it didn't land. Instead it remained a few feet above the ground, with its engines running. Even though the ground crew held the blimp steady with long ropes, it still moved around. I had to leap onto the stairway leading to the gondola.

Once inside the glass-enclosed gondola, I was comforted when I saw the two pilots, who appeared confident and relaxed. The dashboard was lit up with gauges and filled with switches. There were enough seats for six passengers. I chose a seat near the pilots and quickly latched my seat belt. Every passenger on board had a window seat. The windows on a blimp are much larger than the ones on jet airplanes. I could tell that this blimp was made for sightseeing.

As soon as everyone was seated, the pilots took the blimp to a height of about 2,500 feet. The best part of the ride was the view. Because blimps usually cruise at about 3,000 feet, or one-tenth the height at which jets cruise, I could see things in detail. I could see traffic jams, people in swimming pools, and sculptures in open-air malls. The blimp flew over a football game for several minutes, and I could read the player's numbers! Since the cabin is not pressurized, I was able to open my window and wave to the people in the stands.

Once the pilots could see that their passengers were comfortable with their surroundings, they asked us if we were interested in learning more about the workings of a blimp. The pilots explained that the inside of the blimp's outer skin, or envelope, is filled with thousands of cubic feet of helium. Helium is lighter than air. When the helium in the envelope rises, it causes the blimp to ascend. Inside the envelope are two *ballonets*, one in front and one in back. These air-filled sacs help maintain the shape of the envelope. The pilots let air into or out of the ballonets during the flight to keep the pressure balanced in the envelope. The pilots demonstrated this to us. As the blimp gained altitude, helium pressure against the envelope increased. So the pilots let air out of the ballonets. Then, as the pilots moved the blimp downward to decrease altitude, the helium pressure against the envelope decreased. The pilots then let air into the ballonets.

After a short question-and-answer session with the pilots, we headed back to the airport. The pilots were in contact with the blimp's ground crew to make sure that they were ready for docking. As we approached the airfield, I thought about the *Hindenburg* as it prepared to dock on that fateful day in 1937. I reminded myself that helium, unlike hydrogen, is nonflammable. This helped calm me enough so that I could watch our docking. I counted 13 crew members on the field. They grabbed the two ropes that dangled from the nose of the blimp. I unbuckled my seat belt, thanked the pilots, and leaped out of the gondola and onto the ground.

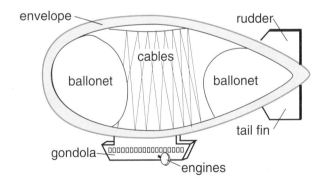

GO ON

4 What is the main idea of the first paragraph?

A The *Hindenburg* was one of the largest airships ever built.

B The *Hindenburg* was classified as a rigid airship.

C The *Hindenburg* held hydrogen gas in its hull.

D The *Hindenburg* disaster ended the development of rigid airships.

5 You can tell that the word *apprehensive* means—

F nervous.

G daring.

H clever.

J humorous.

6 You can tell from this article that the author views blimps with—

A affection.

B apprehension.

C confidence.

D indifference.

7 How did the author get into the gondola of the blimp?

_____

_____

_____

_____

_____

_____

_____

8 Which expresses an *opinion* in the article?

F The gondola on the blimp was glass-enclosed.

G The best part of the blimp ride was the view.

H Blimps cruise at about 3,000 feet.

J A blimp's outer skin is called the envelope.

9 In this article, the author's fear of docking may have been caused by—

A the question-and-answer session with the pilots.

B the lack of ground crew members.

C ropes dangling from the nose of the blimp.

D knowledge of the *Hindenburg* disaster.

10 Which of these is a *fact* stated in the article?

F Helium is nonflammable.

G The pilots were confident.

H People thought the *Hindenburg* was the greatest airship.

J The author enjoyed waving to the people at the football game.

11 What is the purpose of ballonets on a blimp?

_____

_____

_____

_____

_____

_____

_____

_____

GO ON ➡

Answers

4 Ⓐ Ⓑ Ⓒ Ⓓ   6 Ⓐ Ⓑ Ⓒ Ⓓ   9 Ⓐ Ⓑ Ⓒ Ⓓ

5 Ⓕ Ⓖ Ⓗ Ⓙ   8 Ⓕ Ⓖ Ⓗ Ⓙ   10 Ⓕ Ⓖ Ⓗ Ⓙ

Gorillas—An Endangered Species

Gorillas are one of the many endangered species that live in Africa. These large fascinating apes are in danger of extinction for several reasons. As the human population of Africa grows, more land is needed for farmland. The rain forests where the gorillas live are being cut down to make new farms. In some regions, gorillas are hunted for meat.

Western Lowland Gorilla

There are three distinct groups of gorillas in Africa. The western lowland gorillas live in far west Africa near the equator. They make up the largest group, numbering between 35,000 and 45,000 individuals. These apes live in lowland forests and are mainly threatened by loss of habitat, as forests are cut down to make farms. Most gorillas in zoos are from western Africa.

Eastern Lowland Gorilla

The eastern lowland gorillas live in the eastern Democratic Republic of the Congo. There are about 3,000 to 5,000 gorillas in this region. Like the western lowland gorillas, they are also threatened by the loss of their habitat. Poachers are another threat to the gorillas because the poachers roam the region, setting traps for deerlike animals called *duikers.* The poachers bend bamboo stalks and tie them to the ground. Then they attach a wire loop to the bamboo. When an animal steps into the loop, the bamboo springs up and jerks the animal off the ground. Often a gorilla can pull itself free from the trap, but the wire remains around its leg. The wound often becomes dirty and infected, causing the gorilla to sicken and die.

Mountain Gorilla

Mountain gorillas live in a small region on the border between Rwanda, Uganda, and the Democratic Republic of the Congo. They live in an area 25 miles long and about 10 miles wide in the Virunga Mountains. Of the three kinds of gorillas, the mountain gorillas are the most endangered. There are fewer than 400 individuals left in the wild.

There is an encouraging side to the story of the mountain gorillas in Rwanda. Their home is protected because it is part of Rwanda's National Park of the Volcanoes. Because poachers were killing many gorillas, several large organizations banded together in 1978 to form the Mountain Gorilla Project. Its goals were to protect the park and to stop poaching. The project also aimed to increase tourism and to educate local people about gorillas.

Since 1978 the number of gorillas in the park has increased from 240 to nearly 300. Tourists from all over the world have come to see the gorillas. Trackers and tourist guides lead tourists deep into the mountains to observe the small bands of apes in their natural surroundings. Increased tourism has created jobs for many people in Rwanda. Tourism also provides money that can be used to catch poachers. The Mountain Gorilla Project teaches people about the value of the forest to the gorillas that live there.

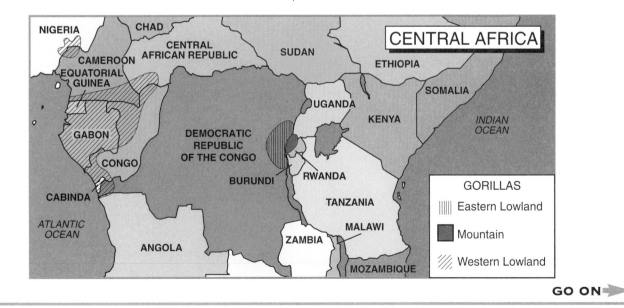

GO ON

12 This article would *most* likely be found in—

A an English textbook.

B a biography.

C a nature magazine.

D a science-fiction novel.

13 The web shows some important ideas in the article.

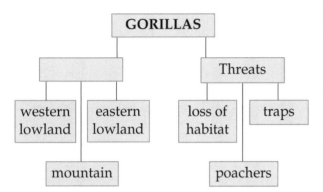

Which of these belongs in the empty space?

F Reasons

G Groups

H Projects

J Resources

14 Why are traps set for duikers dangerous to gorillas?

A The wire from the trap wounds the gorilla, causing death.

B Most gorillas cannot get out of the traps and they starve to death.

C The gorillas are shot by poachers when they are found in the traps.

D The traps poison the gorillas.

15 According to the map, where do the eastern lowland gorillas live?

F in Rwanda

G in Uganda

H in Burundi

J in the Democratic Republic of the Congo

16 Several large organizations banded together to form the Mountain Gorilla Project because—

A there were only five mountain gorillas left in the wild.

B many gorillas were being killed by poachers.

C gorillas were needed for zoos.

D scientists wanted to visit the mountains and study the gorillas.

17 The last paragraph informs the reader—

F about the habitat of the mountain gorilla.

G about Rwanda's National Park of the Volcanoes.

H about interactions between the eastern and western lowland gorillas.

J about the success of the Mountain Gorilla Project.

18 Why is the rapidly growing human population in Africa a threat to the gorillas?

_____

_____

_____

_____

GO ON

Answers

12 Ⓐ Ⓑ Ⓒ Ⓓ   **14** Ⓐ Ⓑ Ⓒ Ⓓ   **16** Ⓐ Ⓑ Ⓒ Ⓓ

13 Ⓕ Ⓖ Ⓗ Ⓙ   **15** Ⓕ Ⓖ Ⓗ Ⓙ   **17** Ⓕ Ⓖ Ⓗ Ⓙ

Jack's Night to Cook

On a hot summer day, nothing beats the flavor of spicy ground beef mixed with cheese, salsa, and cool vegetables. Jack located his favorite cookbook, *Simple Gourmet Cookbook,* and found the recipes he wanted to make. By following the instructions carefully, he made a delicious, well-balanced meal for himself and his family.

Super Taco Salad *(serves 4)*

Ingredients:

1 head lettuce

1 cucumber

1 pound ground beef

1 pinch cumin

1 15-ounce can of beans (kidney, black, green, or pinto)

2 medium tomatoes, diced

2 or 3 green onions, chopped

$1\frac{1}{2}$ cups tortilla chips

$1\frac{2}{3}$ cups cheese, grated (either Monterey jack or mild cheddar)

$\frac{1}{4}$ cup sour cream (optional)

$\frac{1}{4}$ cup salad dressing (see page 97)

$\frac{1}{4}$ cup salsa (see page 105)

Wash the lettuce and break into bite-size pieces in a large bowl. Peel and slice the cucumber, dice the tomatoes, and chop the green onions. Grate the cheese and add it to the bowl with the vegetables, beans, and tortilla chips.

Brown the ground beef in a skillet, stirring over medium heat. Add a pinch of cumin. Remove the pan from the stove after the meat has lost its pink color, but before it gets crispy. Drain the meat and add it to the salad.

Add the salad dressing, and toss the salad well. For a spicier flavor, blend in the salsa. Finally, add the sour cream and garnish the top of the salad with more tortilla chips.

Salsa

Ingredients:

2 ripe tomatoes, diced

1 small onion, chopped fine

$\frac{1}{2}$ teaspoon finely chopped chiles (fresh or canned)

Salt and pepper to taste

Dice the tomatoes, and chop the onions and chiles. Combine all ingredients in a small bowl.

Salad Dressing

Ingredients:

In a small bowl or jar, combine the following–

1 teaspoon lemon juice or vinegar

3 tablespoons olive oil or vegetable oil

$\frac{1}{4}$ teaspoon dry mustard (optional)

Salt and pepper to taste

Mix or shake ingredients to blend. Refrigerate. Shake well before using.

GO ON

19 Jack needs all the following things to make the Super Taco Salad *except*—

A a fork.

B a skillet.

C a can opener.

D a grater.

20 Which ingredient does Jack need in order to make both the taco salad and the salsa?

F cheese

G green onions

H tomatoes

J chiles

21 How much cheese should Jack add to the taco salad?

A $1\frac{1}{2}$ cups

B $1\frac{1}{4}$ teaspoons

C $1\frac{2}{3}$ cups

D $\frac{1}{3}$ teaspoon

22 What is the first thing Jack does when making the taco salad?

F grates the cheese

G opens the can of beans

H washes the lettuce

J slices the cucumber

23 According to the recipe, when should Jack add the salad dressing to the taco salad?

A before he browns the ground beef

B after he garnishes the salad with tortilla chips

C after he adds the meat to the salad

D before he adds the beans to the salad

24 How does Jack prepare the green onions for the taco salad?

F He slices them.

G He chops them.

H He browns them.

J He grates them.

25 If Jack discovers he is out of olive oil, what can he use instead?

A vinegar

B vegetable oil

C lemon juice

D dry mustard

26 What should Jack do just after he adds the salad dressing to the salad?

F Shake the jar.

G Add more lemon juice.

H Stir it over medium heat.

J Toss the salad well.

27 Where can Jack find the recipe for salad dressing in *Simple Gourmet Cooking*?

A page 24

B page 97

C page 105

D page 211

28 Why are these recipes good for a hot summer day?

_____

_____

_____

_____

GO ON

Answers

19 Ⓐ Ⓑ Ⓒ Ⓓ   **21** Ⓐ Ⓑ Ⓒ Ⓓ   **23** Ⓐ Ⓑ Ⓒ Ⓓ   **25** Ⓐ Ⓑ Ⓒ Ⓓ   **27** Ⓐ Ⓑ Ⓒ Ⓓ

20 Ⓕ Ⓖ Ⓗ Ⓙ   **22** Ⓕ Ⓖ Ⓗ Ⓙ   **24** Ⓕ Ⓖ Ⓗ Ⓙ   **26** Ⓕ Ⓖ Ⓗ Ⓙ

Attic Finds

My brother Paul and I helped our mom clean out the attic the other day. We hoped to find a shoe box full of baseball cards from the 1960s that our dad collected when he was about our age. We figured that if the cards were in perfect condition, they might be worth hundreds of dollars.

The first box that we came upon contained holiday decorations that my great-grandmother had given my mother years ago. Every one of the decorations was handmade, and we marveled at the amount of time it must have taken to make each one. Mom had stories about some of the pieces—tales passed down to her by her grandmother.

Finally we found a shoe box that fit the description that Dad had given us. I undid the rubber band so fast that it shot into the other side of the attic. What I found inside wasn't what I had hoped for and expected, but something more valuable to our family than cards of baseball celebrities. I discovered a shoe box full of yellowing letters. The bottom of each page had an odd typed message, "Help our country by saving. Write on BOTH sides of this paper." The top of each paper had a United States flag in the upper left-hand corner, a triangle with the letters *YMCA* in the upper right-hand corner, and the typed words *With the Colors* in the middle of the page. Upon further inspection, Paul and I realized that we had a collection of letters written by our great-uncle Frank while he served as a bugler in the United States Army during World War I. His letters started in boot camp in 1917 and ended in France in 1918. Paul and I spent the rest of the day mulling over the letters.

29 The author assumes the reader already knows—

F why he and his brother are cleaning the attic.

G who gave his mother the holiday decorations.

H what a boot camp is.

J when the letters were written.

30 Why was the message put on the bottom of each page of the letters?

_____

_____

_____

_____

_____

_____

_____

31 Based on the article, you can tell that the author probably—

A threw away the letters.

B read each letter.

C left the letters in the attic.

D sold the letters to a collector.

32 The third paragraph tells mainly—

F what baseball cards were found in the box.

G about finding something unexpected in an attic.

H why World War I started.

J how the United States Army won World War I.

UNIT 4
READING VOCABULARY

=====DETERMINING WORD MEANINGS=====

Directions: Darken the circle for the word or group of words that has the same or almost the same meaning as the underlined word.

| TRY THIS | Choose your answer carefully. The other choices may seem correct. Be sure to think about the meaning of the underlined word. |

Sample A

To <u>transmit</u> is to—

A   imprint   C   interpret

B   design   D   send

| THINK IT THROUGH | The correct answer is <u>D</u>, "send." Transmit means "send." It doesn't mean imprint, design, or interpret. |

STOP

1   Something that is <u>adjacent</u> is—

A   crumbling   C   neighboring

B   locked   D   illegal

2   <u>Conspicuous</u> means—

F   invisible   H   adequate

G   considerate   J   obvious

3   A <u>caress</u> is a kind of—

A   soap   C   touch

B   cloth   D   word

4   Something that is <u>hazardous</u> is—

F   guarded   H   scenic

G   chemical   J   perilous

5   A <u>rebellion</u> is—

A   a border   C   an uprising

B   a conference   D   an organization

6   To <u>merge</u> is to—

F   unite   H   obstruct

G   veer   J   anticipate

7   Someone who is in <u>agony</u> is in—

A   traction   C   great pain

B   sadness   D   a forest

8   To <u>categorize</u> is to—

F   classify   H   analyze

G   describe   J   respond

9   <u>Vast</u> is the same as—

A   green   C   enormous

B   wild   D   settled

10   To <u>veto</u> is to—

F   forbid   H   suggest

G   like   J   order

STOP

Answers

SA Ⓐ Ⓑ Ⓒ ⬤   3 Ⓐ Ⓑ Ⓒ Ⓓ   6 Ⓕ Ⓖ Ⓗ Ⓙ   9 Ⓐ Ⓑ Ⓒ Ⓓ

1 Ⓐ Ⓑ Ⓒ Ⓓ   4 Ⓕ Ⓖ Ⓗ Ⓙ   7 Ⓐ Ⓑ Ⓒ Ⓓ   10 Ⓕ Ⓖ Ⓗ Ⓙ

2 Ⓕ Ⓖ Ⓗ Ⓙ   5 Ⓐ Ⓑ Ⓒ Ⓓ   8 Ⓕ Ⓖ Ⓗ Ⓙ

Directions: Darken the circle for the sentence that uses the underlined word in the same way as the sentence in the box.

TRY THIS

Read the sentence in the box. Decide what the underlined word means. Then find the sentence in which the underlined word has the same meaning.

Sample A

> What is the current temperature?

In which sentence does current have the same meaning as it does in the sentence above?

A The river's strong current washed the pier away.

B Our class discusses current events.

C The current of the oceans creates a pattern across the face of the earth.

D How is an electric current produced?

THINK IT THROUGH

The correct answer is B. In choice B and in the sentence in the box, current means "present."

STOP

1
> The date of the next track meet is March 5, 1998.

In which sentence does date have the same meaning as it does in the sentence above?

A Scientists use carbon dating to date fossils.

B Will Mary be Jesse's date for the dance?

C The date palm produces a sweet fruit.

D What is today's date?

2
> Megan was elected class delegate.

In which sentence does delegate have the same meaning as it does in the sentence above?

F Our state delegate just resigned.

G The teacher will delegate two students to make copies of the program.

H The Constitution provides for citizens to delegate power to their elected representatives.

J You need to delegate some of your responsibilities to others.

3
> During a depression many people lose their jobs.

In which sentence does depression have the same meaning as it does in the sentence above?

A The boulder that fell from the cliff made a depression in the ground.

B He often suffers from depression.

C The depression you see is the result of a meteor that crashed to the earth.

D When the depression ended, the economy started improving.

4
> Where is the river's outlet?

In which sentence does outlet have the same meaning as it does in the sentence above?

F Please find the electrical outlet.

G You need an outlet for your energy.

H The mud slide blocked the outlet from the campground.

J Let's shop at the new shoe outlet.

STOP

Answers

SA Ⓐ ● Ⓒ Ⓓ   1 Ⓐ Ⓑ Ⓒ ●   2 ● Ⓖ Ⓗ Ⓙ   3 Ⓐ Ⓑ Ⓒ ●   4 Ⓕ Ⓖ ● Ⓙ

Directions: Darken the circle for the word or words that give the meaning of the underlined word.

> **TRY THIS**
>
> Read the first sentence carefully. Look for clue words in the sentence. Then use each answer choice in place of the underlined word. Be sure that your answer and the underlined word have the same meaning.

Sample A

During the strike the factory was empty, and the machines were <u>idle</u>. <u>Idle</u> means—

A busy   C occupied

B operating   D inactive

THINK IT THROUGH

The correct answer is <u>D</u>. **Idle** means "inactive." The clue words are "empty" and "strike." The three other choices mean the opposite of <u>idle</u>.

 STOP

---

1 Nurse Gibbons praised Kyle for being a very <u>efficient</u> hospital volunteer. <u>Efficient</u> means—

A talkative   C irritating

B capable   D slow

2 To prevent infection, it is extremely important that hospitals be <u>hygienic</u>. <u>Hygienic</u> means—

F organized   H sanitary

G charitable   J thrifty

3 Alexandra felt <u>annoyed</u> because she was tired of waiting in the slow cafeteria line. <u>Annoyed</u> means—

A afraid   C fearless

B silly   D bothered

4 The students voted to <u>abolish</u> the unpopular dress code. <u>Abolish</u> means—

F preserve   H promote

G eliminate   J hide

5 The man was convicted for his <u>reprehensible</u> acts. <u>Reprehensible</u> means—

A courageous   C thoughtful

B disgraceful   D courteous

6 The <u>rustler</u> was a hated figure in the Wild West. <u>Rustler</u> means—

F cattle thief   H ranch hand

G sheriff   J cowboy

7 At the climax of the movie, the hero faced his deadly <u>adversary</u>. <u>Adversary</u> means—

A friend   C enemy

B companion   D leader

8 Alyssa loves the incredible stories about <u>mythical</u> figures. <u>Mythical</u> means—

F imaginary   H strange

G heroic   J military

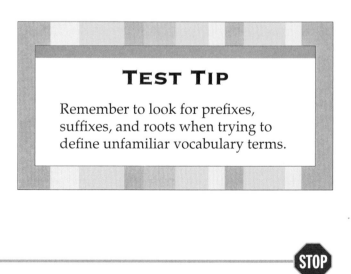

TEST TIP

Remember to look for prefixes, suffixes, and roots when trying to define unfamiliar vocabulary terms.

STOP

Answers

SA Ⓐ Ⓑ Ⓒ ●   2 Ⓕ Ⓖ ● Ⓙ   4 Ⓕ ● Ⓗ Ⓙ   6 Ⓕ ● Ⓗ Ⓙ   8 ● Ⓖ Ⓗ Ⓙ

1 Ⓐ ● Ⓒ Ⓓ   3 Ⓐ Ⓑ Ⓒ ●   5 Ⓐ ● Ⓒ Ⓓ   7 Ⓐ Ⓑ ● Ⓓ

Sample A

To <u>convey</u> is to—

A build

B transport

C examine

D memorize

 STOP

For questions 1–8, darken the circle for the word or group of words that has the same or almost the same meaning as the underlined word.

1 To <u>defy</u> is to—

A expose

B support

C challenge

D excuse

2 <u>Absurd</u> means—

F admirable

G confused

H forgotten

J ridiculous

3 A <u>replica</u> is—

A an experiment

B a secret code

C an exact copy

D a priceless antique

4 Something that is <u>amiss</u> is—

F filthy

G satisfactory

H lost

J wrong

5 <u>Dense</u> means—

A thick

B smoky

C dirty

D dangerous

6 An <u>inquiry</u> is—

F a delivery

G an identity

H an investigation

J a route

7 A <u>pamphlet</u> is a kind of—

A teacher

B academy

C newspaper

D booklet

8 To <u>allay</u> is to—

F put at rest

G discuss in public

H make fun of

J imagine

Write your answer for the following:

9 What is the meaning of the word <u>aroma</u>?

_____

_____

TEST TIP

Be precise when writing word definitions. Use the formal language you might find in a dictionary.

GO ON ➡

Answers
SA Ⓐ Ⓑ ● Ⓓ   2 Ⓕ Ⓖ ⬤ Ⓙ   4 Ⓕ ⬤ Ⓗ Ⓙ   6 Ⓕ Ⓖ Ⓗ Ⓙ   8 ⬤ Ⓖ Ⓗ Ⓙ
1 Ⓐ Ⓑ Ⓒ ⬤   3 Ⓐ Ⓑ Ⓒ Ⓓ   5 ⬤ Ⓑ Ⓒ Ⓓ   7 Ⓐ Ⓑ Ⓒ Ⓓ

Sample B

> The hiker tried to <u>scale</u> the mountain.

In which sentence does <u>scale</u> have the same meaning as it does in the sentence above?

A   Find the distance <u>scale</u> on the map.

B   He can easily <u>scale</u> that wall.

C   The doctor carefully placed the newborn baby on the <u>scale</u>.

D   What is the pay <u>scale</u> for this job?

For questions 10–14, darken the circle for the sentence in which the underlined word means the same as it does in the sentence in the box.

10
> Kaitlin is helping Rodney build a new <u>pen</u> for the cattle.

In which sentence does <u>pen</u> have the same meaning as it does in the sentence above?

A   How did the pigs get out of their <u>pen</u>?

B   May I please borrow your <u>pen</u>?

C   Where is Dad going to <u>pen</u> the sheep?

D   Why did that author <u>pen</u> such an awful book?

11
> There was a <u>remote</u> possibility that she was telling the truth.

In which sentence does <u>remote</u> have the same meaning as it does in the sentence above?

F   Where did you put the <u>remote</u> control?

G   He is a <u>remote</u> ancestor of mine.

H   The house was located in a <u>remote</u> part of town.

J   They had a <u>remote</u> chance of winning the contest.

12
> The teacher will <u>marshal</u> the children out of the building.

In which sentence does <u>marshal</u> have the same meaning as it does in the sentence above?

A   He was once a federal <u>marshal</u>.

B   It would be best to <u>marshal</u> your arguments in order of importance.

C   She is the new city fire <u>marshal</u>.

D   <u>Marshal</u> them into a single file.

13
> Dad helped me <u>review</u> for the Spanish test.

In which sentence does <u>review</u> have the same meaning as it does in the sentence above?

F   The general requested a <u>review</u> of the troops before the ceremony.

G   He wrote a very glowing <u>review</u> of her latest novel.

H   The musical <u>review</u> was a great success.

J   The detectives met to <u>review</u> the events that led to the crime.

14
> Mom can <u>maneuver</u> the car through heavy traffic easily.

In which sentence does <u>maneuver</u> have the same meaning as it does in the sentence above?

A   Pilots learn to <u>maneuver</u> their planes in emergency situations.

B   The movement of thousands of troops in an hour was a huge <u>maneuver</u>.

C   The soldiers practiced the <u>maneuver</u> all weekend.

D   She can <u>maneuver</u> her way out of any uncomfortable situation.

GO ON

Answers
SB   Ⓐ ⬤ Ⓒ Ⓓ   11   Ⓕ Ⓖ Ⓗ ⬤   13   Ⓕ Ⓖ Ⓗ ⬤
10   ⬤ Ⓑ Ⓒ Ⓓ   12   Ⓐ Ⓑ Ⓒ ⬤   14   ⬤ Ⓑ Ⓒ Ⓓ

Sample C

The cost for the car repair was <u>trivial</u>.
<u>Trivial</u> means—

A insignificant

B significant

C important

D expensive

STOP

For questions 15–22, darken the circle for the word or words that give the meaning of the underlined word.

15 The detectives were totally <u>baffled</u> by the lack of clues in the case. <u>Baffled</u> means—

F puzzled

G rewarded

H amused

J relaxed

16 Carol tried to remain <u>neutral</u> while her two friends argued. <u>Neutral</u> means—

A giving advice

B not taking sides

C perfectly still

D whistling

17 Tree limbs and branches scattered by the storm <u>obstructed</u> the entrance to the park. <u>Obstructed</u> means—

F blocked

G signaled

H opened

J decorated

18 Dale was coughing and sneezing, and he felt altogether <u>miserable</u>. <u>Miserable</u> means—

A energetic

B starved

C unhappy

D generous

19 My dog Skipper is <u>notorious</u> for chewing anything, but he is especially fond of shoes. <u>Notorious</u> means—

F pampered

G remorseful

H abnormal

J well-known

20 Many people leave their countries to escape political <u>oppression</u>. <u>Oppression</u> means—

A freedom

B benefits

C persecution

D reliability

21 That <u>scoundrel</u> stole the widower's life savings. What is the meaning of the word <u>scoundrel</u>?

_____

_____

_____

22 It is important that the researchers keep a <u>sanitary</u> laboratory. What is the meaning of the word <u>sanitary</u>?

_____

_____

_____

_____

STOP

Answers

SC Ⓐ Ⓑ Ⓒ ●   **16** Ⓐ Ⓑ Ⓒ Ⓓ   **18** Ⓐ Ⓑ Ⓒ Ⓓ   **20** Ⓐ Ⓑ Ⓒ Ⓓ

15 Ⓕ Ⓖ Ⓗ Ⓙ   **17** Ⓕ Ⓖ Ⓗ Ⓙ   **19** Ⓕ Ⓖ Ⓗ Ⓙ

MATH PROBLEM-SOLVING PLAN

OVERVIEW

THE PROBLEM-SOLVING PLAN

When solving math problems follow these steps:

STEP 1: WHAT IS THE QUESTION/GOAL?

Read the problem. Decide what must be found. This is sometimes in the form of a question.

STEP 2: FIND THE FACTS

Locate the factual information:
   A. KEY FACTS are the facts you need to solve the problem.
   B. FACTS YOU DON'T NEED are those facts which are not necessary for solving the problem.
   C. ARE MORE FACTS NEEDED? Decide if you have enough information to solve the problem. If not, what information would you need or what assumptions could you make to arrive at a conclusion?

STEP 3: SELECT A STRATEGY

Decide what strategies you might use, how you will use them, and in what form you will offer your solution. For example, will you present your solution numerically, in words, in a chart or diagram, or in some other way? If one strategy doesn't help you to solve the problem, try another.

STEP 4: SOLVE

Apply the strategy according to your plan. Communicate your solution in a clear and accurate fashion.

STEP 5: DOES YOUR RESPONSE MAKE SENSE?

Think about your solution. Read the problem again. Check to see that your answer makes sense. Use estimation to check calculations.

Directions: Use the problem-solving plan to solve this math problem.

PROBLEM/QUESTION:

Migdalia is a consultant. She works 3 days a week in the company's headquarters and 2 days a week at a production site. When she works at the company headquarters, she takes a bus to and from work. When she goes to production sites, she uses her car and travels 52 miles per day. The cost for using the bus is $48.00 for 10 one-way trips. The cost of using her car she estimates at 30¢ per mile. Migdalia budgets $50 per week for travel expenses to and from work. Show whether or not she has set aside enough money.

STEP 1: WHAT IS THE QUESTION/GOAL?

_____

_____

STEP 2: FIND THE FACTS

_____

_____

STEP 3: SELECT A STRATEGY

_____

_____

STEP 4: SOLVE

_____

_____

STEP 5: DOES YOUR RESPONSE MAKE SENSE?

_____

_____

_____

_____

_____

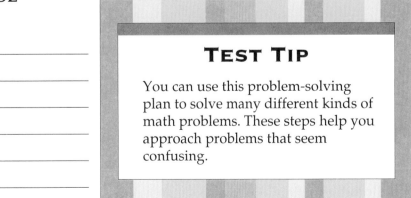

TEST TIP

You can use this problem-solving plan to solve many different kinds of math problems. These steps help you approach problems that seem confusing.

Directions: Use the problem-solving plan to solve this math problem.

PROBLEM/QUESTION:

Alberto has an L-shaped room shown in the diagram at the right. He has purchased a square piece of carpeting that has an area of 30 sq. yds. Approximately what percent of the carpet he purchased will be left over?

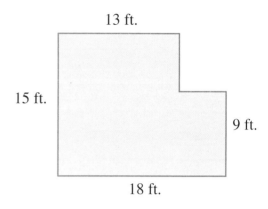

STEP 1: WHAT IS THE QUESTION/GOAL?

_____

_____

_____

STEP 2: FIND THE FACTS

_____

_____

_____

STEP 3: SELECT A STRATEGY

_____

_____

_____

STEP 4: SOLVE

_____

_____

_____

STEP 5: DOES YOUR RESPONSE MAKE SENSE?

_____

_____

_____

_____

MATH PROBLEM SOLVING

UNDERSTANDING NUMBER THEORY

Directions: Darken the circle for the correct answer, or write in your answer.

TRY THIS — Read each question twice before choosing your answer. Be sure to think about which numbers stand for ones, tens, hundreds, and so on.

Sample A

Which fraction is smallest in value?

A $\frac{1}{8}$ C $\frac{3}{5}$

B $\frac{1}{5}$ D $\frac{3}{8}$

THINK IT THROUGH The correct answer is <u>A</u>. The fraction $\frac{1}{8}$ is smaller than the other fractions listed. If you use the common denominator 40, $\frac{1}{8}$ becomes $\frac{5}{40}$, but the other fractions become $\frac{8}{40}$, $\frac{4}{40}$, and $\frac{15}{40}$.

STOP

---

1   Oceanographers estimate that the Atlantic Ocean covers 4.1×10^7 square miles, expressed in scientific notation. What is another way that number can be written?

A   410 square miles

B   41,000 square miles   41,00,0,000

C   410,000 square miles

D   41,000,000 square miles

2   What is the value of point B on the number line?

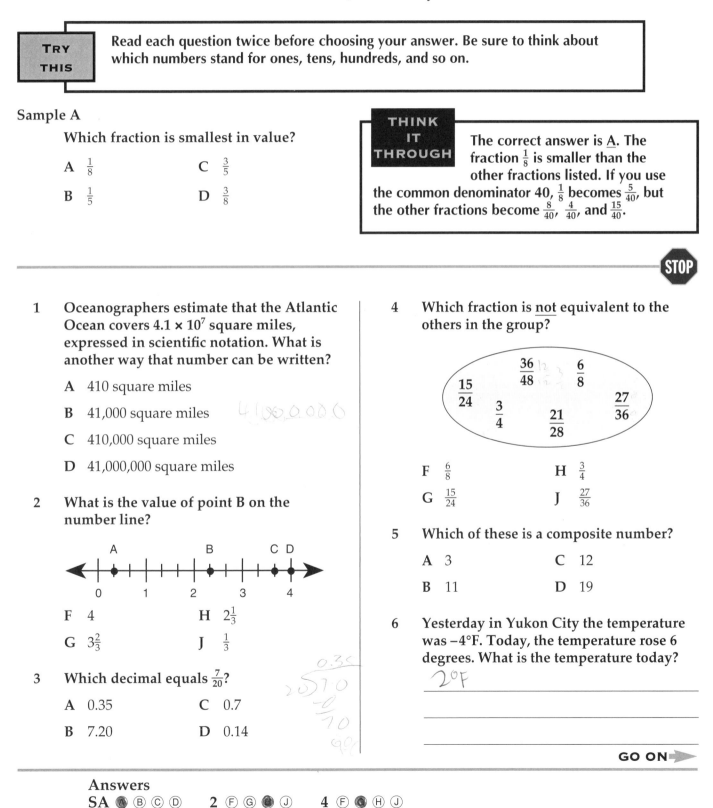

F   4   H $2\frac{1}{3}$

G $3\frac{2}{3}$ J $\frac{1}{3}$

3   Which decimal equals $\frac{7}{20}$?

A   0.35   C   0.7

B   7.20   D   0.14

4   Which fraction is <u>not</u> equivalent to the others in the group?

F $\frac{6}{8}$ H $\frac{3}{4}$

G $\frac{15}{24}$ J $\frac{27}{36}$

5   Which of these is a composite number?

A   3   C   12

B   11   D   19

6   Yesterday in Yukon City the temperature was −4°F. Today, the temperature rose 6 degrees. What is the temperature today?

2°F

GO ON

Answers

SA Ⓐ Ⓑ Ⓒ Ⓓ   2 Ⓕ Ⓖ Ⓗ Ⓙ   4 Ⓕ Ⓖ Ⓗ Ⓙ

1 Ⓐ Ⓑ Ⓒ Ⓓ   3 Ⓐ Ⓑ Ⓒ Ⓓ   5 Ⓐ Ⓑ Ⓒ Ⓓ

7 Maddy saw this sign when she was shopping. What is the value of the 5 in the sale price of men's ties?

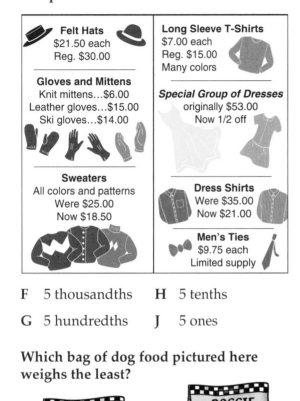

Felt Hats
$21.50 each
Reg. $30.00

Long Sleeve T-Shirts
$7.00 each
Reg. $15.00
Many colors

Gloves and Mittens
Knit mittens…$6.00
Leather gloves…$15.00
Ski gloves…$14.00

Special Group of Dresses
originally $53.00
Now 1/2 off

Sweaters
All colors and patterns
Were $25.00
Now $18.50

Dress Shirts
Were $35.00
Now $21.00

Men's Ties
$9.75 each
Limited supply

F 5 thousandths   **H** 5 tenths

G 5 hundredths   **J** 5 ones

8 Which bag of dog food pictured here weighs the least?

DOGGIE YUM $4\frac{5}{8}$ LB.
Bag A

DOGGIE GRUB $4\frac{2}{3}$ LB.
Bag C

GRADE A DOG CHOW $4\frac{7}{12}$ LB.
Bag B

GOURMET DOG FOOD $4\frac{3}{4}$ LB.
Bag D

A Bag A   **C** Bag C

B Bag B   **D** Bag D

9 Which number is <u>not</u> a prime number?

F 11

G 17

H 27

J 31

10 Each ☐ represents 0.001. Which number is represented in the picture shown here?

A 12.5

B 1.25

C 0.125

D 0.0125

11 Which scale is correctly balanced?

F 2^3 3^2

G 5^3 3^5

H 8^2 4^3

J 6^2 2^6

STOP

Answers

7 Ⓕ ⬤ Ⓗ Ⓙ   **8** Ⓐ ⬤ Ⓒ Ⓓ   **9** Ⓕ Ⓖ ⬤ Ⓙ   **10** Ⓐ Ⓑ ⬤ Ⓓ   **11** Ⓕ Ⓖ ⬤ Ⓙ

Directions: Darken the circle for the correct answer, or write in your answer.

TRY THIS

Check your work by making sure both sides of an equation are equal values. Try using all the answer choices in the problem.

Sample A

If $x > y$ and $y > z$, then

A $x < z$

B $x \geq z$

C $x = z$

D $x > z$

THINK IT THROUGH

The correct answer is <u>D</u>. If x is greater than y, and y is greater than z, it is logical that x is also greater than z.

 STOP

---

1 Holly is making 2 kinds of necklaces. For one, she uses blue beads. For the other, she uses green beads. She needs 32 beads for each necklace. If she has 300 blue beads and 200 green beads, which number sentence could be used to determine the maximum number of necklaces she can make?

A $(300 \div 32) + (200 \div 32) = \square$

B $300 + 200 + 32 = \square$

C $(300 \geq \square) = 32$

D $(300 - 200) \div 32 = \square$

2 If $5 > y$, which number could <u>not</u> be a value for y?

F -4

G 2

H 4

J 5

3 Which expression demonstrates that 12 less than x equals 40?

A $12 \div x = 40$

B $12 - x = 40$

C $40 - 12 \leq x$

D $x - 12 = 40$

4 Mei baked a German chocolate cake. She knows that the cake contains 2,700 calories. She has cut the cake into 12 equal-size slices. Write an equation to determine the number of calories in each slice.

$2700 \div 12 =$ 225

$12\overline{)2700}$
24
30
24
60

5 Mr. Lopez bought 3 boxes of cereal for $2.65 each. He bought 6 cartons of orange juice for $0.89 each. Which number sentence could be used to determine how much money Mr. Lopez spent altogether?

F $(3 \times \$2.65) + (6 \times \$0.89) = \square$

G $(\$2.65 + \$0.89) \times (3 + 6) = \square$

H $(3 \times 6) + (\$2.65 \times \$0.89) = \square$

J $(3 + \$2.65) \times (6 + \$0.89) = \square$

 STOP

Answers

SA Ⓐ Ⓑ Ⓒ ●   1 ● Ⓑ Ⓒ Ⓓ   2 Ⓕ Ⓖ Ⓗ ●   3 Ⓐ Ⓑ Ⓒ ●   5 ● Ⓖ Ⓗ Ⓙ

Directions: Darken the circle for the correct answer, or write in your answer.

TRY THIS

Read each problem carefully. Determine the nature of the pattern or relationship in the problem. Try using all the answer choices in the problem to find the correct solution.

Sample A

Rodney is saving money to buy his first car. His parents agreed to contribute 50 cents for every dollar he saved. If he has saved $1,100, how much can he afford to spend on the car?

A $1,450

B $1,650

C $2,300

D $3,450

THINK IT THROUGH

The correct answer is B. If Rodney has saved $1100, then his parents are contributing half of the $1,100, or $550. Therefore, Rodney can afford to spend $1,100 + $550, or $1,650, on the car.

STOP

---

1 A special machine multiplies any number entered into it by 8. The table shows how numbers are changed. Which numbers are missing from the table? Write them in the empty boxes.

Original number	5	7	10
New number	40	56	80

2 If 3 teaspoons of baking powder are required for a batch of 8 pancakes, how much baking powder will be needed for a batch of 32 pancakes?

A 6 teaspoons

B 8 teaspoons

C 9 teaspoons

D 12 teaspoons

TEST TIP

Use scratch paper to extend patterns and check your answers.

3 Look at the part of Pascal's Triangle shown here. If the pattern continues, the next line would be _____.

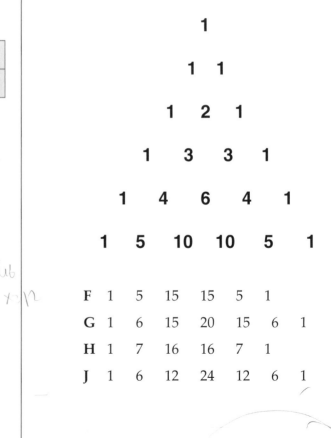

```
              1
            1   1
          1   2   1
        1   3   3   1
      1   4   6   4   1
    1   5  10  10   5   1
```

F 1   5   15   15   5   1

G 1   6   15   20   15   6   1

H 1   7   16   16   7   1

J 1   6   12   24   12   6   1

STOP

Answers
SA ⒶⒷⒸⒹ   2 ⒶⒷⒸⒹ   3 ⒻⒼⒽⒿ

Directions: Darken the circle for the correct answer, or write in your answer.

TRY THIS

Read each question twice before choosing your answer. Study any given tables or graphs to help you choose the correct answer.

Sample A

Two coins are tossed into the air. What is the probability that they will match either heads-heads or tails-tails when they land?

A $\frac{1}{1}$

B $\frac{1}{2}$

C $\frac{1}{4}$

D $\frac{1}{8}$

THINK IT THROUGH

The correct answer is <u>B</u>. There are four possibilities: heads-heads, tails-tails, heads-tails, and tails-heads. Two of these four possibilities will match. That makes the correct answer a probability of $\frac{2}{4}$, or $\frac{1}{2}$.

STOP

1 The graph depicts the rainfall in a city over a 12-month period.

Annual Rainfall

Which of these statements is true, based on the information in the graph?

A There were 18 inches of rainfall during the 12-month period shown on the graph.

B It rained 2 inches in December.

C There was more rainfall in April and in May than in the rest of the months combined.

D There was less rainfall in November than in any other month of the year.

2 The graph shows the results of a student vote taken to select the music for a school dance.

If 600 students voted, how many voted for rock music?

F 560

G 340

H 240

J 142

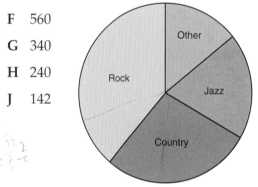

3 A consumer organization surveyed the cost of milk at local grocery stores. At Store A, the cost of a gallon of milk was $2.49. At Store B, it was $2.29. At Store C it was $2.75, and at Store D it was $2.19. Using these prices, what is the average (mean) cost of a gallon of milk?

A $9.72   C $2.53

B $3.63   D $2.43

GO ON

Answers

SA Ⓐ ● Ⓒ Ⓓ   1 ● Ⓑ Ⓒ Ⓓ   2 Ⓕ Ⓖ ● Ⓙ   3 Ⓐ Ⓑ Ⓒ ●

A stem-and-leaf chart is an easy method of organizing data from a list.

Stem	Leaf
15	2, 4, 6
16	2, 3

means

152, 154, 156
162, 163

The stem-and-leaf chart below shows the finishing times (in seconds) for the 100-meter dash at a recent middle school track meet. Use the chart to answer questions 4 through 6.

Finishing Times (in seconds)	
Stem	**Leaf**
12	8, 9
13	6, 7, 9, 9
14	2, 8
15	2, 7

4 Which tally chart shows the correct number of students whose time was less than 130 seconds?

120 - 130	II
130 - 140	IIII
140 - 150	III
150 - 160	I

F

120 - 130	III
130 - 140	IIII
140 - 150	III
150 - 160	III

H

120 - 130	III
130 - 140	IIII
140 - 150	I
150 - 160	II

G

120 - 130	III
130 - 140	IIII
140 - 150	III
150 - 160	II

J

5 What is the probability that a student's time was less than 140 seconds?

A $\frac{1}{10}$ C $\frac{2}{5}$

B $\frac{1}{4}$ D $\frac{3}{5}$

6 How many students had a finishing time greater than 137 seconds?

F 8   H 6

G 7   J 5

7 Tanya made each point on the scatter plot represent test results. The coordinates for each point show the hours she studied for the test and the grade she received.

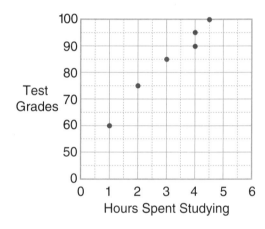

How many hours did Tanya study to receive a grade of 90?

4

8 If 45 out of 100 people said that they read the newspaper every day, how many people out of 500 would be expected to read one every day?

STOP

Directions: Darken the circle for the correct answer, or write in your answer.

TRY THIS

Use the objects shown to help you answer each question. Remember that circumference and perimeter are the measurements around the outside of a figure, while area and volume are the measurements of the inside of a figure.

Sample A

What is the volume of a packing box 10 inches long, 8 inches wide, and 12 inches high?

A   30 in³

B   80 in³

C   920 in³

D   960 in³

THINK IT THROUGH

The correct answer is D, 960 in³. To determine the volume of a rectangular prism, multiply length by width by height: 10 × 8 × 12 = 960 in³.

STOP

1   What is the area of the shaded portion of triangle ABC? (Use A = ½bh)

A   6 square units

B   8 square units

C   12 square units

D   24 square units

2   Which three-dimensional figure has exactly five faces?

F   cube

G   triangular prism

H   rectangular prism

J   cylinder

3   The new conference table is shown here. What is the approximate area of the table? (Use A = πr² and π = 3.14.)

A   78.5 sq ft

B   49.29 sq ft

C   34.85 sq ft

D   15.7 sq ft

4   A sandbox measures 8 centimeters by 5 centimeters by 10 centimeters. How much sand is required to fill the box?

GO ON

Answers
SA Ⓐ Ⓑ Ⓒ ●   1 Ⓐ Ⓑ Ⓒ Ⓓ   2 Ⓕ Ⓖ Ⓗ Ⓙ   3 Ⓐ Ⓑ Ⓒ Ⓓ

5 The diameter of circle X is represented by which line segment?

F $\overline{AX}$

G $\overline{BX}$

H $\overline{AB}$

J $\overline{AC}$

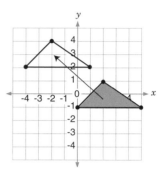

6 Which coordinates best represent the last point needed to complete the vertices of a rectangle?

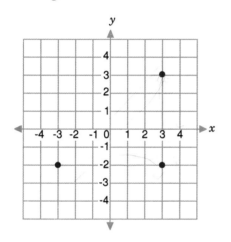

A (-2, -2)

B (-3, 3)

C (-2, 2)

D (2, 2)

7 Which of these figures shows line m perpendicular to line n?

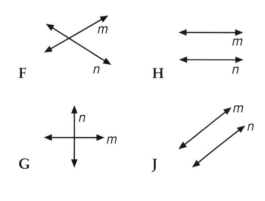

8 The light figure shows where the dark figure will be after it slides the direction shown by the arrow.

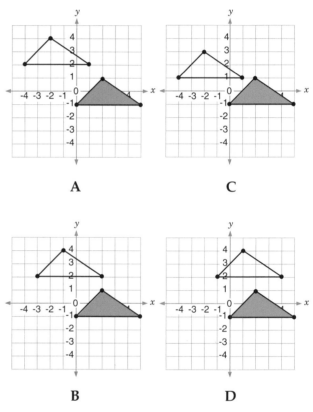

Which of the following shows the same slide?

A

C

B

D

9 A stone sundial has a diameter of 30 inches. What is the approximate circumference of the sundial? (Use $C = 2\pi r$ and $\pi = 3.14$.)

_____

_____

_____

_____

STOP

Answers

5 F G H ● 6 ● B C D 7 F ● H J 8 ● B C D

70

Directions: Darken the circle for the correct answer, or write in your answer.

TRY THIS Study all the answer choices carefully. Sometimes more than one answer looks correct. Study any given visuals to help you choose your answer.

Sample A

What is the approximate length of line ST shown here?

S ●━━━━━━━━━━● T

A 4 meters

B 4 centimeters

C 4 kilometers

D 4 millimeters

THINK IT THROUGH

The correct answer is B, 4 centimeters. Both 4 kilometers and 4 meters measure much longer than line ST, and 4 millimeters measures much shorter than line ST.

STOP

---

1 Which of these is closest to the measure of the angle between the top of the cactus and the ground?

A 90°

B 80°

C 50°

D 30°

2 The runway at the county airport measures 2,300 meters long. How many kilometers long is that?

F 230 kilometers

G 23 kilometers

H 2.3 kilometers

J 0.23 kilometers

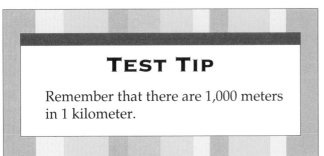

TEST TIP

Remember that there are 1,000 meters in 1 kilometer.

3 Use the map scale to help answer this question. According to the map, what is the shortest distance by railroad from Faramin to Oakton?

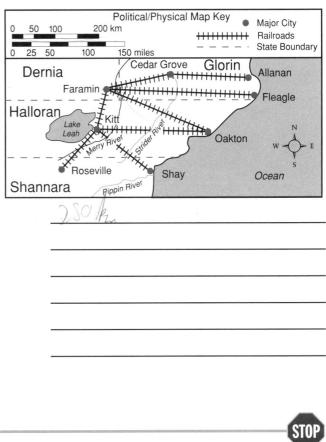

250 km

STOP

Directions: Darken the circle for the correct answer.

TRY THIS

Round numbers when you estimate. For some problems, there are no exact answers. Then you should take your best guess. You can check your answer by using the numbers given in the problem.

Sample A

Mrs. Rubin's garden store had 527 rosebushes. She sold 215 of them. Which is the best estimate of the number of rosebushes she has left?

A 400

B 300

C 200

D 100

THINK IT THROUGH

The correct answer is <u>B</u>. Start by rounding 527 rosebushes to 500. Then round 215 to 200. You couldn't have 400, 200, or 100 left. Check by subtracting 200 from 500. The best estimate is <u>300</u>.

STOP

---

1 Akiko bought $5\frac{2}{3}$ yards of imported silk at $7.98 yard. She plans to use $3\frac{1}{2}$ yards of the silk to make a dress. About how much material will Akiko have left?

A $1\frac{5}{8}$ yards   C 3 yards

B 2 yards   D $3\frac{1}{2}$ yards

2 Martina bought craft supplies that totaled $47.58. If the sales tax is 8%, which is the best estimate of the tax Martina paid?

F $3.00   H $9.89

G $4.00   J $15.78

3 A sculptor makes a scale drawing of a statue he is sculpting. If he wants the statue to be 50 feet tall, and he uses paper the size of this page, which is a reasonable scale for his drawing?

A 1 inch represents 10 feet

B 1 inch represents 1 foot

C $\frac{1}{2}$ inch represents 1 foot

D $\frac{1}{8}$ inch represents 1 foot

4 Benjamin started with 3.18 kilograms of flour. He used 664 grams to make a cake. The best estimate of the amount of flour he has left in grams is *about*—

F 1,000 grams   H 2,300 grams

G 1,500 grams   J 4,000 grams

5 A baby-sitting service charges $1.75 per child per hour. *About* how much would a family pay the service to baby-sit 3 of their children for 6 hours?

A $9.50   C $18.00

B $12.00   D $36.00

6 The scale on a map of New Jersey shows that 4 inches equals 25 miles. The distance from Newark to Atlantic City measures 14.2 inches on the map. *About* how many miles does that represent?

F less than 40 miles

G between 80 and 90 miles

H between 100 and 110 miles

J more than 115 miles

STOP

Answers

SA Ⓐ ● Ⓒ Ⓓ   2 ● Ⓖ Ⓗ Ⓙ   4 Ⓕ Ⓖ ● Ⓙ   6 Ⓕ ● Ⓗ Ⓙ

   1 Ⓐ ● Ⓒ Ⓓ   3 Ⓐ Ⓑ Ⓒ Ⓓ   5 Ⓐ Ⓑ Ⓒ ●

Directions: Darken the circle for the correct answer, or write in your answer.

TRY THIS Study the words in each problem carefully. Then decide what you have to do to find the answer.

Sample A

Lina makes decorative pillows. She can sew a pillow in 25 minutes. What additional information is needed to find how long it takes Lina to sew an entire set of pillows?

A the length of each pillow

B the weight of each pillow

C the cost of the materials

D the number of pillows in a set

THINK IT THROUGH The correct answer is <u>D</u>. You do not need to know the length or weight of each pillow, nor the cost of the materials. To find out how long it takes to make a *set*, you need to know how many pillows are in a set.

STOP

1 How many non-straight angles can you find in this figure?

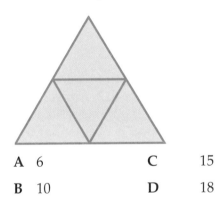

A 6 C 15

B 10 D 18

2 All of Sam's friends like to play chess. Some of his friends like to play checkers. None of Sam's friends likes to play bridge. Perry, who is the school chess champion, also likes to play bridge. Which of the following statements must be true?

F Sam and Perry are friends.

G Perry plays checkers.

H Sam plays bridge.

J Sam and Perry are not friends.

3 What can be done to Side A to balance the scale? Each cube equals $1\frac{1}{2}$ cylinders.

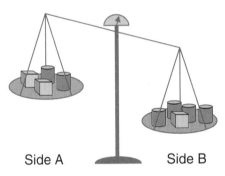

Side A   Side B

A Remove one cube and add one cylinder.

B Remove one cylinder and add one cube.

C Add two cylinders.

D Remove two cylinders and add one cube.

4 Chuck's birthday is 2 days before Linus's. Lucy's birthday is 3 days after Marcy's. Patty's birthday is 4 days before Lucy's. If Marcy's birthday is March 10, when is Patty's birthday?

_____

_____

GO ON

Answers

SA Ⓐ Ⓑ Ⓒ Ⓓ   1 Ⓐ Ⓑ Ⓒ Ⓓ   2 Ⓕ Ⓖ Ⓗ Ⓙ   3 Ⓐ Ⓑ Ⓒ Ⓓ

5 The sum of the first two numbers in Max's apartment number is twice the sum of the last two numbers. Which of these could be Max's apartment number?

F 842

G 824

H 428

J 248

6 The price offered per pound for cattle was $7.89. The first cow weighed 1,289.6 pounds, the second cow weighed 1,065.2 pounds, and the third weighed 1,134.07 pounds. Which of these questions <u>cannot</u> be answered using the information given?

A What is the total weight of the cattle?

B How much weight did the heaviest cow gain in one year?

C How much weight difference is there between the lightest and the heaviest cow?

D What is the total price paid for the 2 heaviest cows?

7 There are 13 students in one lunch line and 29 students in the other lunch line. How many students would need to move from the long line to the short line to make both lines equal?

_____

_____

_____

_____

8 There were 72 children at the picnic. If they were organized into 6 even softball teams, how many children were on each team?

_____

_____

_____

_____

Use the picture shown here to answer questions 9 and 10. Each rectangular prism is equal to 2 cylinders.

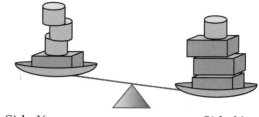

Side X   Side Y

9 If 1 cylinder equaled 3 rectangular prisms, which of the following would be true?

F Side X > Side Y

G Side X < Side Y

H Side X = Side Y

J Side X ≈ Side Y

10 What should be added to Side X so that the scales balance?

A 2 rectangular prisms

B 1 rectangular prism and 1 cylinder

C 2 cylinders

D 1 cylinder

11 Alexa bought a beach towel for $11, a beach umbrella for $12, and sunscreen for $7. She paid for the items with a $50 bill. What information is <u>not</u> needed to find out how much Alexa paid for her purchases?

F The beach towel costs $11.

G The beach umbrella costs $12.

H The sunscreen costs $7.

J She paid with a $50 bill.

TEST TIP

Remember that *not* is an important signal word in a question.

STOP

Sample A

Which fraction is smallest in value?

A $\frac{3}{8}$

B $\frac{3}{10}$

C $\frac{7}{10}$

D $\frac{1}{2}$

🛑 STOP

For questions 1–45, darken the circle for the correct answer, or write in your answer.

1 Light travels at a speed of 186,282 miles per second. How could this distance be expressed using scientific notation?

A $1,862.82 \times 10^3$

B 186.282×10^{-3}

C 1.86282×10^4

D 1.86282×10^5

2 Which point best represents 7.8 on the number line?

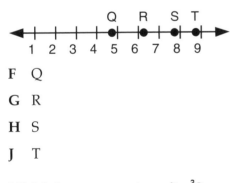

F Q

G R

H S

J T

3 Which is <u>not</u> a way to write $\frac{3}{4}$?

A 0.75%

B 0.75

C $\frac{75}{100}$

D 75%

4 What is the value of the 4 in the number 872.0654?

F 4 tenths

G 4 hundredths

H 4 ten-thousandths

J 4 hundred-thousandths

5 Which decimal shows the part of the figure that is shaded?

A 00.58   C 5.8

B 0.58   D 5.80

6 Which of the following numbers is greater than -1?

F 0   H -3

G -2   J -4

7 Which fraction is equivalent to $\frac{6}{9}$?

A $\frac{2}{3}$ C $\frac{3}{9}$

B $\frac{3}{6}$ D $\frac{4}{8}$

8 Which number listed here is <u>not</u> a prime number?

F 9   H 7

G 11   J 5

GO ON ➡

Answers
SA Ⓐ Ⓑ Ⓒ Ⓓ   2 Ⓕ Ⓖ Ⓗ Ⓙ   4 Ⓕ Ⓖ Ⓝ Ⓙ   6 Ⓕ Ⓖ Ⓗ Ⓙ   8 Ⓕ Ⓖ Ⓗ Ⓙ
1 Ⓐ Ⓑ Ⓒ Ⓓ   3 Ⓐ Ⓑ Ⓒ Ⓓ   5 Ⓐ Ⓑ Ⓒ Ⓓ   7 Ⓐ Ⓑ Ⓒ Ⓓ

9 The mystery number M is 5 more than twice the value of 12. Which number sentence could be used to find the value of M?

  A $M = (12 \div 2) - 5$

  B $M = (12 \times 2) + 5$

  C $M = 12 + (2 \times 5)$

  D $M = 5 + 2 + 12$

10 Lena bought 8 ounces of walnuts. If the walnuts sell for $1.25 a pound, which number sentence could be used to find P, the price Lena paid for the walnuts?

  F $\$1.25 \div 2 = P$

  G $(8 + 8) \times \$1.25 = P$

  H $\$1.25 \div 8 = P$

  J $(\$1.25 \div 2) \times 8 = P$

11 Which of the scales shown here is correctly balanced?

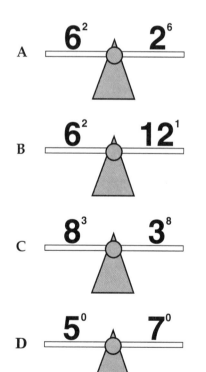

A 6^2 2^6

B 6^2 12^1

C 8^3 3^8

D 5^0 7^0

12 Which expression demonstrates that 8 multiplied by y equals 120?

  F $\frac{8}{y} = 120$

  G $120 \times 8 = y$

  H $8y = 120$

  J $120 > \frac{y}{8}$

13 Choose the symbol that makes this statement true.
$7\frac{7}{12} \underline{\quad} 7\frac{5}{11}$

  A $\geq$

  B $<$

  C $=$

  D $>$

14 Which expression means the same as $15 \times n - 2$?

  F $15n - 2$

  G $15(n - 2)$

  H $15 - n - 2$

  J $13n$

15 For every pound Miguel lifts in a weight-lifting contest, his sponsor will contribute $3 to Miguel's college savings. If Miguel lifts 350 pounds, how much will his sponsor contribute?

_____

_____

16 There is one ripe tomato in a garden. With tomorrow as the first day, the number of ripe tomatoes in the garden increases by three each day. If this pattern continues, how many ripe tomatoes would be produced on the fifteenth day?

_____

_____

_____

GO ON ➡

17 It is Celina's turn in a board game she is playing with her friends. What is the probability that Celina will lose a turn on this spin?

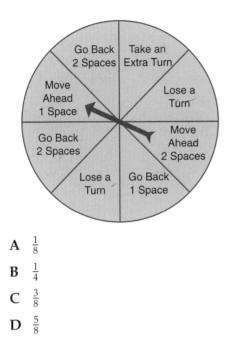

A $\frac{1}{8}$

B $\frac{1}{4}$

C $\frac{3}{8}$

D $\frac{5}{8}$

Use the menu below to answer question 18.

Malcolm's Coffee Shop

Drinks		Desserts	
Coffee	$0.85	Cake	$1.85
Milk	$0.55	Cheesecake	$1.45
Orange Juice	$0.65	Donuts	$0.95

18 How many beverage-and-dessert combinations could possibly be ordered at Malcolm's Coffee Shop?

F 3

G 6

H 9

J 12

19 A special machine multiplies any number entered into it by 9. The table shows how numbers are changed. Which numbers complete the table? Write them in the empty boxes.

Original number	4	6	9
New number	36	54	81

This graph shows the number of students who walked to school during a certain week. Use the graph to answer question 20.

20 What is the average (mean) number of students who walked to school during this week?

GO ON ➡

Answers

The "stem" in this chart is the *tens* digit in the ages. The "leaf" is the *ones* digit in the ages.The stem-and-leaf chart below shows the ages of members of a hiking club.

Use the chart to answer questions 21 through 23.

Mountain Hiking Club	
Stem	**Leaf**
1	7, 7, 8, 9
2	1, 2, 2, 2, 4
3	0, 3, 3, 5
4	1, 1, 4, 5, 7
5	0, 3

21 How many 22-year-olds are members of the hiking club?

A 5

B 4

C 3

D 2

22 What is the probability that a member chosen at random is a teenager?

F $\frac{4}{5}$

G $\frac{2}{5}$

H $\frac{3}{10}$

J $\frac{1}{5}$

23 If one of the members made a tally chart showing the number of members in each category, how many tally marks would be in the 30 – 40 row?

A 4

B 5

C 8

D 9

24 The graph shows 500 responses to the question, "How would you spend a prize of $10,000?" How many of the 500 would use the prize money as a down payment on a house?

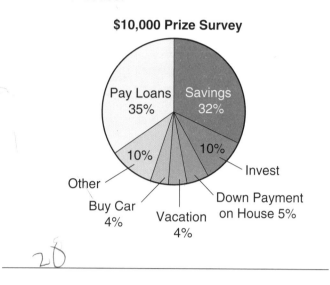

$10,000 Prize Survey

25 About what percent of students in Grade 7 play music after school?

Use the graph below to answer questions 25 and 26.

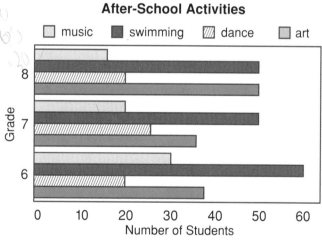

After-School Activities

25 About what percent of students in Grade 7 play music after school?

F 60%   H 30%

G 45%   J 15%

26 About what percent of students in Grade 6 swim after school?

A 20%   C 60%

B 40%   D 100%

GO ON ➡

Answers

21 Ⓐ Ⓑ Ⓒ Ⓓ   **22** Ⓕ Ⓖ Ⓗ Ⓙ   **23** Ⓐ Ⓑ Ⓒ Ⓓ   **25** Ⓕ Ⓖ Ⓗ Ⓙ   **26** Ⓐ Ⓑ Ⓒ Ⓓ

27 Which transformation moves the figure from position A to position B?

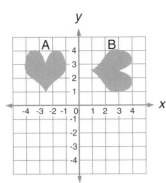

F   extension

G   rotation

H   reflection

J   translation

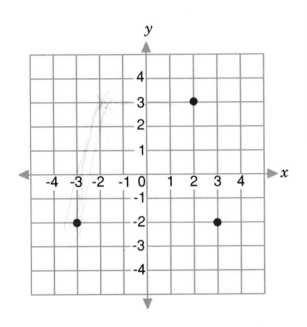

28 Which coordinates best represent the last point needed to complete the vertices of a trapezoid?

A   (-2, -3)

B   (-2, -2)

C   (-2, 3)

D   (3, -3)

29 How many faces does this figure have?

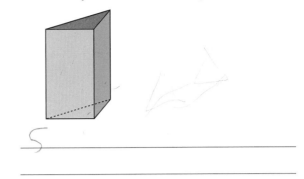

_____

_____

_____

30 Pam's mother stores buttons in this wood box. What is the volume of the box?

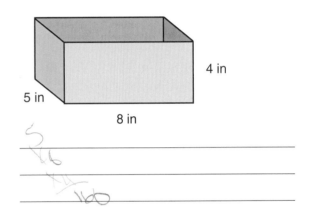

4 in

5 in

8 in

_____

_____

_____

A student wanted to see if the hours spent watching television relate to scores on a test.

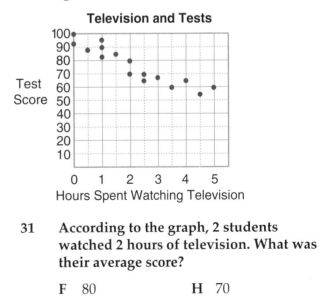

Television and Tests

Test Score

Hours Spent Watching Television

31 According to the graph, 2 students watched 2 hours of television. What was their average score?

F   80   H   70

G   75   J   65

GO ON ➡

Answers

27 Ⓕ ⓖ Ⓗ Ⓙ   **28** Ⓐ Ⓑ ⓒ Ⓓ   **31** Ⓕ Ⓖ Ⓗ Ⓙ

32 Which 2 line segments are parallel in the figure shown here?

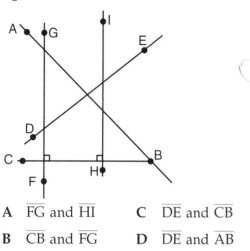

A $\overline{FG}$ and $\overline{HI}$ C $\overline{DE}$ and $\overline{CB}$

B $\overline{CB}$ and $\overline{FG}$ D $\overline{DE}$ and $\overline{AB}$

33 Use your centimeter ruler to answer this question. What is the area of the triangle shown here? (Use $A = \frac{1}{2}bh$.)

F 3 cm^2 H 4.5 cm^2

G 3.5 cm^2 J 5 cm^2

34 A football player kicked a football 45.5 feet. How long was the kick in yards and inches?

A 2 yards 13 inches

B 3 yards 9 inches

C 12 yards 3 inches

D 15 yards 6 inches

35 What is the diameter of the circle shown here?

F 2 inches

G 3 inches

H 10 inches

J 12 inches

36 The diameter of this pizza is 14 inches. What is the circumference? (Use $C = 2\pi r$ and $\pi = 3.14$.)

A 10.99 inches

B 21.98 inches

C 43.96 inches

D 307.72 inches

37 Members of the science class want to build a scale model of the space shuttle. If the space shuttle is approximately 122 feet in length, 57 feet high, and has a wingspan of 78 feet, which is a reasonable scale for the model?

F 1 inch represents 20 feet

G 1 inch represents 100 feet

H $\frac{1}{2}$ inch represents 1 foot

J $\frac{1}{2}$ inch represents 100 feet

38 The KTCW television station in Cody has a viewing area that ranges 150 miles from Cody. Which town on the map cannot receive KTCW broadcasts?

GO ON →

Answers

32 ● Ⓑ Ⓒ Ⓓ   34 Ⓐ Ⓑ Ⓒ ●   36 Ⓐ Ⓑ ● Ⓓ

33 Ⓕ Ⓖ Ⓗ Ⓙ   35 Ⓕ Ⓖ Ⓗ ●   37 Ⓕ ● Ⓗ Ⓙ

80

39 Kyle has earned 40% of the money he needs to buy a used car. If the selling price of the car is $7,850, *about* how much more money does Kyle need to buy the car?

  A $2,500

  B $3,000

  C $4,000

  D $5,000

40 East Willow Town was founded in 1875. The population has grown over the years. What information is <u>not</u> needed to find out how much the population has grown?

  F the population in 1875

  G how many babies have been born in East Willow Town

  H how many people have moved to East Willow Town

  J how many towns have been founded in the state

Use the scale shown here to answer question 41. Each cone weighs 2 kilograms.

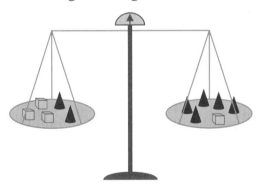

41 What is the weight of 1 cube?

  A 1.5 kilograms

  B 2 kilograms

  C 3 kilograms

  D 3.5 kilograms

42 Allen drank $\frac{2}{3}$ of a pint of water in the morning, $1\frac{1}{4}$ pints in the afternoon, and $1\frac{1}{3}$ pints in the evening. Which is closest to the total amount of water Allen drank?

  F 14 ounces

  G 5 cups

  H $3\frac{1}{2}$ quarts

  J 1 gallon

43 Chris is older than his brother Sam. Ralph is older than Sam, but younger than Chris. Sam is also younger than Ben. Chris is not the oldest. What is the correct order of the brothers from youngest to oldest?

  A Sam, Ralph, Chris, Ben

  B Sam, Ben, Ralph, Chris

  C Sam, Chris, Ralph, Ben

  D Ben, Chris, Sam, Ralph

44 There were four cross-country team members running in an event. Robin finished after Earl. Nick finished after Robin. Neal finished ahead of Robin but after Earl. Which of the following shows the order in which the runners finished the event from first to last?

  F Earl, Neal, Robin, Nick

  G Neal, Earl, Robin, Nick

  H Robin, Earl, Nick, Neal

  J Nick, Robin, Neal, Earl

45 Candace collected the most money for the fund raiser. Randy collected $14 more than Gina, but $22 less than Candace. If Gina collected $98, then how much did Candace collect?

STOP

Answers

Directions: Darken the circle for the correct answer. Darken the circle for NH (Not Here) if the correct answer is not given.

TRY THIS

Check the answer to a division problem by multiplying. Multiply the answer by the smaller number in the problem. That answer should equal the larger number in the problem.

Sample A

$1{,}440 \div 12 =$

A 112
B 102
C 144
D 120
E NH

THINK IT THROUGH

The correct answer is D, 120. Check this by multiplying. Since $120 \times 12 = 1{,}440$, you know the answer is correct.

STOP

1

$8 \times \frac{3}{4} =$

A $8\frac{3}{4}$
B 6
C 5
D $\frac{3}{4}$
E NH

2

$2\frac{5}{12} + \frac{6}{12} =$

F $2\frac{11}{24}$
G $2\frac{1}{12}$
H $2\frac{11}{12}$
J $2\frac{1}{2}$
K NH

3

$0.28 \times 0.06 =$

A 0.0168
B 0.168
C 1.68
D 1.168
E NH

4

$24.73 + 0.098 =$

F 24.728
G 2.571
H 0.02571
J 25.71
K NH

5

$4 \div \frac{3}{5} =$

A $\frac{3}{20}$
B $\frac{5}{12}$
C $6\frac{2}{3}$
D $2\frac{2}{5}$
E NH

6

$-2 \times -9 =$

F -18
G -11
H -7
J 18
K NH

STOP

Answers
SA Ⓐ Ⓑ Ⓒ Ⓓ Ⓔ   2 Ⓕ Ⓖ ● Ⓙ Ⓚ   4 Ⓕ Ⓖ Ⓗ Ⓙ ●   6 Ⓕ Ⓖ Ⓗ ● Ⓚ
1 Ⓐ ● Ⓒ Ⓓ Ⓔ   3 Ⓐ Ⓑ Ⓒ Ⓓ Ⓔ   5 Ⓐ Ⓑ ● Ⓓ Ⓔ

82

Directions: Darken the circle for the correct answer. Darken the circle in context for NH (Not Here) if the correct answer is not given, or write in the answer.

TRY THIS

Read the word problem carefully. Then set up the word problem as a numerical formula. Solve the formula, and compare your answer with the answer choices.

Sample A

A bookcase has 4 shelves and contains 168 books. If the books are evenly divided on the shelves, how many books are there on each shelf?

A 40
B 172
C 164
D 42
E NH

THINK IT THROUGH

To find how many books are on one shelf, divide the number of books by the number of shelves. Since 168 ÷ 4 = 42, the answer is D.

STOP

---

1 Mariah spent half of her allowance for a gift. She then deposited $4.50 into her savings account and spent the remaining $6.00 bowling. What percent of her allowance did Mariah put into savings?

A 21.4%

B 28.5%

C 50%

D 78.5%

E NH

2 If Esteban swims the same distance every day, and he swims $10\frac{1}{2}$ miles in two weeks, how many miles does he swim each day?

F $1\frac{1}{4}$ miles

G $\frac{7}{8}$ miles

H $\frac{3}{4}$ miles

J $\frac{2}{3}$ miles

K NH

3 The Fox family is driving 1,500 miles. They drove 475 miles yesterday and 520 miles today. How many more miles will they drive?

A 995 miles

B 505 miles

C 2,495 miles

D 45 miles

E NH

4 The Canoe Club took 72 adults and 12 students on a trip. Each bus held 24 people. How many buses were there?

GO ON

Answers
SA Ⓐ Ⓑ Ⓒ Ⓓ Ⓔ   1 Ⓐ Ⓑ Ⓒ Ⓓ Ⓔ   2 Ⓕ Ⓖ Ⓗ Ⓙ Ⓚ   3 Ⓐ Ⓑ Ⓒ Ⓓ Ⓔ

5 Maurice made $4\frac{1}{2}$ quarts of gumbo. If one serving is $\frac{1}{4}$ quart, how many servings did Maurice make?

F 18

G 12

H 9

J $5\frac{1}{2}$

K NH

6 Edna has watched 30% of a documentary about meerkats. If she watched 36 minutes of the program, how long is the documentary?

A 1 hour

B $1\frac{1}{2}$ hours

C $2\frac{1}{2}$ hours

D 3 hours

E NH

7 Yesterday it snowed 37.5% of the day. What is that percent rounded to the nearest compatible fraction?

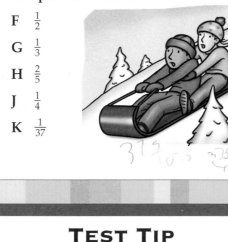

F $\frac{1}{2}$

G $\frac{1}{3}$

H $\frac{2}{5}$

J $\frac{1}{4}$

K $\frac{1}{37}$

TEST TIP

Some trick answers have numbers that only look right. Do not be tricked by $\frac{1}{37}$ in question 7. Be alert for repeated numbers.

---

8 After the party, there were $1\frac{1}{2}$ pepperoni pizzas, $\frac{5}{6}$ of a hamburger pizza, and $\frac{1}{3}$ of a cheese pizza left. What was the total amount of pizza left?

A $\frac{11}{18}$

B $2\frac{1}{6}$

C $2\frac{2}{3}$

D $3\frac{1}{6}$

E $3\frac{1}{2}$

9 The Severn suspension bridge in England is 987.8568 meters long. What is its length rounded to the nearest thousandth?

F 987.857

G 987.9

H 987.856

J 988

K 988.900

10 Darcy earns $4.55 an hour working at the theater in the mall. How much does she make if she works 14 hours this weekend?

STOP

Answers

5 Ⓕ Ⓖ Ⓗ Ⓙ Ⓚ **7** Ⓕ Ⓖ Ⓗ Ⓙ Ⓚ **9** Ⓕ Ⓖ Ⓗ Ⓙ Ⓚ

6 Ⓐ Ⓑ Ⓒ Ⓓ Ⓔ **8** Ⓐ Ⓑ Ⓒ Ⓓ Ⓔ

Sample A

$120 \div 24 =$

A 6
B 5
C 4
D 50
E NH

STOP

Sample B   Socks are packed 5 pairs to a box and 9 boxes to a carton. How many pairs of socks are in a carton?

F 4
G 40
H 14
J 45
K NH

STOP

For questions 1–14, darken the circle for the correct answer. Darken the circle for NH (Not Here) if the correct answer is not given. If there are no choices given, write in you answer.

1
$0.872 - 0.681 =$

A 0.191
B 0.211
C 0.190
D 1.552
E NH

2
$12\frac{5}{7}$
$-\ 5\frac{4}{7}$

F $13\frac{1}{7}$
G $7\frac{9}{7}$
H $7\frac{1}{7}$
J $8\frac{1}{7}$
K NH

3
$8 + {-7} =$

A -15
B 1
C -1
D 15
E NH

4
$\frac{4}{7} \times \frac{3}{7} =$

F $\frac{12}{49}$
G $\frac{3}{4}$
H $1\frac{1}{3}$
J $\frac{7}{14}$
K NH

5
$17.6 - 9.4 =$

A 12.2
B 8.10
C 8.2
D 9.2
E NH

6
$7\frac{2}{3}$
$-\ 10\frac{1}{4}$

F $17\frac{10}{12}$
G $18\frac{1}{2}$
H $17\frac{3}{7}$
J $17\frac{2}{12}$
K NH

7
$2481 \times 285 =$

A 2,766
B 707,085
C 37,215
D 703,485
E NH

8 $\frac{3}{4} \div 6 =$

_____
_____
_____
_____

GO ON

Answers
SA Ⓐ Ⓑ Ⓒ Ⓓ Ⓔ
SB Ⓕ Ⓖ Ⓗ ● Ⓚ
1 ● Ⓑ Ⓒ Ⓓ Ⓔ
2 Ⓕ Ⓖ ● Ⓙ Ⓚ
3 Ⓐ Ⓑ ● Ⓓ Ⓔ
4 ● Ⓖ Ⓗ Ⓙ Ⓚ
5 Ⓐ Ⓑ ● Ⓓ Ⓔ
6 Ⓕ Ⓖ Ⓗ Ⓙ ●
7 Ⓐ Ⓑ Ⓒ Ⓓ ●

9 In Pine Valley there are 5,678 one-story houses and 3,456 two-story houses. How many more one-story than two-story houses are there?

F 1,898

G 2,456

H 2,222

J 2,134

K NH

10 A map was drawn to the scale of 1 cm = 20 miles. If the distance between two cities is $6\frac{1}{2}$ cm, how many miles apart are the two cities?

A $26\frac{1}{2}$ miles

B 120 miles

C 130 miles

D 18 miles

E NH

11 Of the 48 students who signed up for a dance class, only half had dance experience. During the first week, one-third of the inexperienced students dropped the class. How many of the inexperienced students continued taking the dance class?

F 8

G 16

H 24

J 40

K NH

12 Rita and Jack worked on a magazine article. As editor, Jack will receive 60% of the fee. Rita, as photographer, will receive 40% of the fee. If the total fee is $1,200, what will Rita be paid?

A $900

B $720

C $540

D $480

E NH

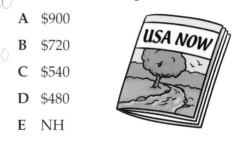

13 Maria scored 19.2 points for her team in two field events—the high jump and the triple jump. She scored 9.4 points in the high jump. How many points did Maria score in the triple jump?

F 9.8

G 10.3

H 0.9

J 9.4

K NH

14 Nicky recently won $12,567 in a raffle. What is that amount rounded to the nearest hundred?

Answers

9 Ⓕ Ⓖ Ⓗ Ⓙ Ⓚ   **11** Ⓕ Ⓖ Ⓗ ● Ⓚ   **13** ● Ⓖ Ⓗ Ⓙ Ⓚ

10 Ⓐ ● Ⓒ Ⓓ Ⓔ   **12** Ⓐ Ⓑ Ⓒ ● Ⓔ

LANGUAGE

PREWRITING, COMPOSING, AND EDITING

Directions: Read each sentence carefully. Then darken the circle for the correct answer to each sentence.

 TRY THIS Imagine you are writing each sentence. Use the rules you have learned for capitalization, punctuation, word usage, and sentence structure to choose the correct answer.

The Costs of Using Tobacco

Celeste is the editor-in-chief of her school newspaper. She knows of several students in her school who smoke or have started smoking. She decides it is important to write an editorial about the hazards of using tobacco.

Sample A

What should Celeste do before she starts to write her editorial?

A Find information about tobacco use.

B Check the spellings of unfamiliar words.

C Make a map showing where tobacco is grown.

D Check a thesaurus to find the best words to use.

 THINK IT THROUGH The correct answer is A. The first thing Celeste should do is find information about her topic. It is important to have a body of factual information to use in order to write a good editorial.

🛑 STOP

While Celeste was writing her editorial, she used the dictionary to check some words.

1 What is the correct way to divide <u>nicotine</u> into syllables?

A ni co tine

B nic o tine

C ni cot ine

D nic ot ine

GO ON ➡

Answers
SA Ⓐ Ⓑ ● Ⓓ   1 ● Ⓑ Ⓒ Ⓓ

Here is a rough draft of the first part of Celeste's editorial. Read the rough draft carefully. Then answer questions 2–9.

The Costs of Using Tobacco

In physical education class, yesterday, Justin collapsed the mile
(1)

while running. Justin used to be one of the best runners on our school's
(2)

track team. What had happened? Was he sick? Had he sprained his
(3)   (4)   (5)

ankle? Did he skip eating breakfast? I had a bowl of oatmeal for
(6)   (7)

breakfast. Everyone wondered what had happened to Justin. I decided
(8)   (9)

to ask him and his answer may surprise you it surprised me.

"I out of breath. My lungs were in extreme pain. I was coughing, and
(10)   (11)   (12)

I lost my energy to run." Justin then admitted that he has been smoking
(13)

cigarettes for the past three months. "I'm only smoking half a pack a
(14)

day. I find it hard to believe that smoking that small amount could
(15)

cause me to feel so bad."

---

2 What is the topic sentence of the first paragraph?

   F 1

   G 2

   H 6

   J 7

3 Which sentence is a run-on sentence?

   A 2

   B 6

   C 7

   D 9

GO ON

Answers
2 ● ⒢ ⒣ ⒥   3 Ⓐ Ⓑ Ⓒ ●

4 How could sentence 1 be correctly rewritten?

Yesterday, in P.E., Justin collapsed while running the mile

5 Which group of words in Celeste's editorial is <u>not</u> a complete sentence?

F 3

G 6

H 10

J 12

6 What is the most colorful way to write sentence 8?

A Everyone wondered why Justin had collapsed.

B Everyone in class wondered what happened to Justin in class to cause his dramatic collapse.

C Everyone wondered what could have happened to Justin in class to make him collapse.

D As it is written.

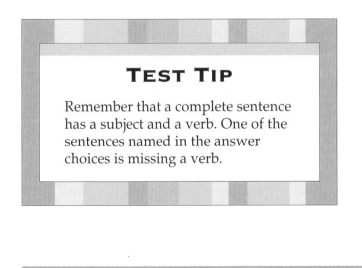

TEST TIP

Remember that a complete sentence has a subject and a verb. One of the sentences named in the answer choices is missing a verb.

7 Combine sentence 10 and sentence 11 into one sentence without changing their meaning.

I'm out of breath and my lungs were in extreme pain.

8 Which of the following sentences could be added after sentence 12?

F Then I just fell to the ground.

G She ran up and tried to stop his fall.

H Celeste writes down everything he says.

J He tripped on his shoelaces.

9 What sentence contains information that does <u>not</u> belong in Celeste's article?

A 5

B 6

C 7

D 12

GO ON ➡

Answers
5 Ⓕ Ⓖ ⬤ Ⓙ   **6** Ⓐ ⬤ Ⓒ Ⓓ   **8** ⬤ Ⓖ Ⓗ Ⓙ   **9** Ⓐ Ⓑ ⬤ Ⓓ

Here is the next part of Celeste's rough draft for her editorial. This part has certain words and phrases underlined. Read the draft carefully. Then answer questions 10–17.

I researched the effects of smoking to find out. Did you knew that
(16)   (17)
the nicotine contained in cigarettes can cause beginning smokers to

become dizzy? Nicotine is a powerful drug. Nicotine made the heart
(18)   (19)
work harder and beat faster.

When they burn, cigarettes release a gas called carbon monoxide.
(20)
This gas causes blood vessels to narrow. It also makes it difficult for
(21)   (22)
your blood cells to carry oxygen to body cells and to carry carbon dioxide

away from the cells to the lungs. Carbon monoxide is the same gas that
(23)
comes out of the exhaust pipes of cars. If you inhale too much of this
(24)
gas, it can kill him.

Another fact that I discovered is that smoking tobacco causes the lungs
(25)
to work less efficiently. Tar, which is a dense, gummy, dark liquid, attaches
(26)
to parts of the respiratory tract, and makes it difficult to breathe properly.

I believe the cost of cigarettes is about $2.00 a pack. That sounds
(27)   (28)
like an expensive habit to me. More costly than this, however, is what
(29)
smoking can cost a person in lost dreams. Justin, is smoking really
(30)
worth losing its ability to run like the wind?

10 In sentence 16, <u>the effects of smoking to find out</u> is best written—

    F smoking effects to find out smoking

    G to find out the effects of smoking

    H the smoking effects to find out

    J As it is written.

11 In sentence 17, <u>you knew that</u> is best written—

    A they knew that

    B you had known

    C you know that

    D As it is written.

12 In sentence 19, <u>Nicotine made the heart</u> is best written—

    F Nicotine makes the heart

    G Nicotine make the heart

    H Nicotine have made the heart

    J As it is written.

13 In sentence 20, <u>When they burn, cigarettes release</u> is best written—

    A When they burned, cigarettes, release

    B When they are burning cigarettes release

    C Cigarettes, when burned release,

    D As it is written.

14 In sentence 24, <u>it can kill him</u> is best written—

    F it can kill her

    G it can kill you

    H it can kill them

    J As it is written.

15 In sentence 26, <u>respiratory tract, and makes it</u> is best written—

    A respiratory, tract, and makes it

    B respiratory tract and, makes it

    C respiratory tract and makes it

    D As it is written.

16 In sentence 26, <u>which is a dense</u> is best written—

    F which was a dense

    G which would have been dense

    H which is densely

    J As it is written.

17 In sentence 30, <u>losing its ability</u> is best written—

    A losing their ability

    B losing your ability

    C losing her ability

    D As it is written.

TEST TIP

Pronouns need to match the case and number of the noun they replace. To answer question 17, reread the sentence to find out what pronoun is needed. Notice that this sentence is directed to Justin. The correct pronoun should be a possessive pronoun in the second person.

STOP

Directions: Read each sentence carefully. If one of the words is misspelled, darken the circle for that word. If all the words are spelled correctly, then darken the circle for *No mistake*.

TRY THIS

Read each sentence carefully. If you are not sure of an answer, first decide which answer choices are spelled correctly. Then see if you can recognize the misspelled word from your reading experience.

Sample A

The lens in the microscope magnifyed the object ten times. No mistake
    A   B   C   D

THINK IT THROUGH

The correct answer is B. Magnified is spelled m-a-g-n-i-f-i-e-d.

STOP

1   We were denied acces to the backstage area at the concert. No mistake
                  A   B   C   D

2   The ornate colums give that house a colonial look. No mistake
               F   G   H   J

3   She is tenseing up before she swings her racket. No mistake
               A   B   C   D

4   We heard the wolf's cry eko throughout the canyon. No mistake
                      F   G   H   J

5   The students were bored by the monatonous speech. No mistake
                      A   B   C   D

6   The pilot made an adjustment before landing the plain. No mistake
              F   G   H   J

7   Did you notice the message on the bulletin board? No mistake
               A   B   C   D

8   Climbing the mountain from this location is not adviseable. No mistake
             F   G   H   J

STOP

Answers
SA Ⓐ ● Ⓒ Ⓓ   2 Ⓕ ● Ⓗ Ⓙ   4 ● Ⓖ Ⓗ Ⓙ   6 Ⓕ Ⓖ ● Ⓙ   8 Ⓕ Ⓖ Ⓗ ●
    1 Ⓐ ● Ⓒ Ⓓ   3 ● Ⓑ Ⓒ Ⓓ   5 Ⓐ ● Ⓒ Ⓓ   7 Ⓐ Ⓑ Ⓒ ●

Sample A

Mara wants to learn to in-line skate. She cannot find a class that teaches this skill. She decides to write a letter to the office of her park district to suggest that the park district offer in-line skating lessons.

Before she writes the letter, Mara wants to know about the success of in-line skating lessons in other park districts. She should look in—

A   an atlas.

B   the *Readers' Guide to Periodical Literature.*

C   a thesaurus.

D   an encyclopedia.

Read the selection below carefully. Then answer questions 1–4.

American Impressionists

In art class Pat learned about impressionism, the style of art that shows what a painter sees at a glance. He was intrigued with the way the impressionists used light and its reflection. He was particularly interested in American impressionists and their contributions to this school of painting. Pat decided to use this as the subject of his research paper for English class.

1   **What should Pat do before he writes his research paper?**

A   check the definitions of words that he might use

B   make an outline of information to include in the paper

C   determine the length of the paper

D   find out what kind of art most people like

2   **Which topic would <u>not</u> be appropriate for Pat's paper?**

F   famous impressionist painters

G   a study of light and color

H   subjects of impressionist paintings

J   how to arrange paintings at an exhibit

3   **Where would Pat find general information about impressionism?**

A   the almanac

B   the dictionary

C   the encyclopedia

D   the thesaurus

4   **Where should Pat look first to find information about American impressionists?**

_____

_____

_____

_____

GO ON ➡

Answers
SA Ⓐ Ⓑ Ⓒ ●   1 Ⓐ ● Ⓒ Ⓓ   2 Ⓕ ● Ⓗ Ⓙ   3 ● Ⓑ Ⓒ Ⓓ

Here is a rough draft of the first part of Pat's research paper. Read the rough draft carefully. Then answer questions 5–10.

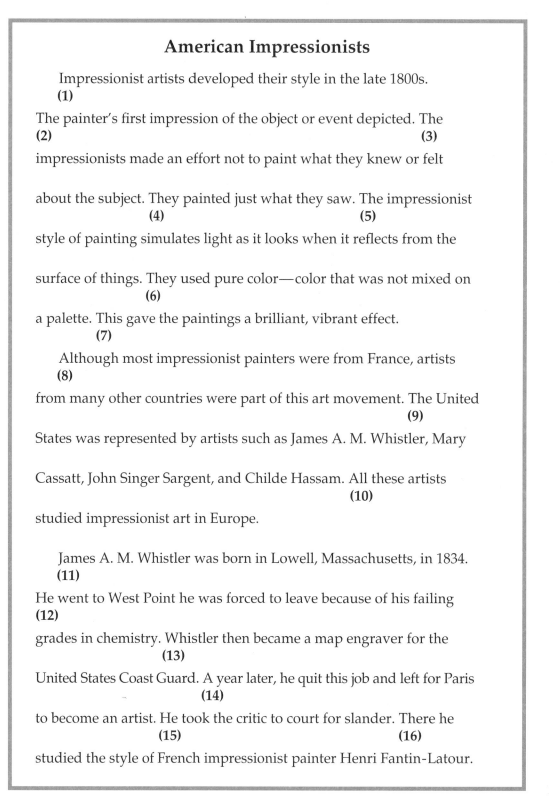

American Impressionists

Impressionist artists developed their style in the late 1800s.
(1)
The painter's first impression of the object or event depicted. The
(2)   (3)
impressionists made an effort not to paint what they knew or felt

about the subject. They painted just what they saw. The impressionist
(4)   (5)
style of painting simulates light as it looks when it reflects from the

surface of things. They used pure color—color that was not mixed on
(6)
a palette. This gave the paintings a brilliant, vibrant effect.
(7)

    Although most impressionist painters were from France, artists
(8)
from many other countries were part of this art movement. The United
(9)
States was represented by artists such as James A. M. Whistler, Mary

Cassatt, John Singer Sargent, and Childe Hassam. All these artists
(10)
studied impressionist art in Europe.

    James A. M. Whistler was born in Lowell, Massachusetts, in 1834.
(11)
He went to West Point he was forced to leave because of his failing
(12)
grades in chemistry. Whistler then became a map engraver for the
(13)
United States Coast Guard. A year later, he quit this job and left for Paris
(14)
to become an artist. He took the critic to court for slander. There he
(15)   (16)
studied the style of French impressionist painter Henri Fantin-Latour.

GO ON ▶

5 Which group of words is <u>not</u> a complete sentence?

   F 2

   G 4

   H 5

   J 6

6 Combine sentences 3 and 4 into one sentence without changing their meaning.

_____

_____

_____

_____

_____

7 Which of the following sentences could be added after sentence 7?

   A Americans did not recognize the artistry of impressionist painters.

   B The impressionist movement lasted for about 50 years.

   C Impressionism can also be found in sculptures.

   D The colors in impressionist paintings often have a shimmering quality to them.

8 Which sentence is a run-on sentence?

   F 6

   G 9

   H 12

   J 13

9 What is the best way to write sentence 11?

   A In 1834, in Lowell, Massachusetts, was born James A. M. Whistler.

   B Lowell, Massachusetts, in 1834, James A. M. Whistler was born.

   C James A. M. Whistler, in Lowell, Massachusetts, in 1834 was born.

   D As it is written.

10 Which sentence contains information that does <u>not</u> belong in this report?

   F 9

   G 10

   H 14

   J 15

TEST TIP

A *run-on sentence* is two or more complete sentences that are incorrectly punctuated to make one sentence.

GO ON ➡

Answers

  5 Ⓕ Ⓖ Ⓗ Ⓙ   **7** Ⓐ Ⓑ Ⓒ Ⓓ   **8** Ⓕ Ⓖ Ⓗ Ⓙ   **9** Ⓐ Ⓑ Ⓒ Ⓓ   **10** Ⓕ Ⓖ Ⓗ Ⓙ

Here is the next part of Pat's rough draft for his research paper. This part has certain words and phrases underlined. Read the draft carefully. Then answer questions 11–18.

Mary Cassatt was born in Allegheny, Pennsylvania, in 1844. She
(17)   (18)

was interested from an early age in painting. Cassatt studies art at the
                                                        (19)

Pennsylvania Academy of Fine Arts. She emigrated to France and she
                                                        (20)

became a well-respected member of the French impressionist movement.

Cassatt's paintings usually depict people doing routine activities. She
(21)   (22)

often chose mothers and children as her subjects. Cassatt used light,
(23)

bright colors and vague brush strokes to create the illusion of what the

eye sees at a glance. She also occasionally used muted colors and strong,
                                                    (24)

clear lines in their paintings. Cassatt encouraged American art collectors
                    (25)

to purchase impressionist paintings. As a result many impressionist
                                            (26)

paintings hang in museum galleries in the United States today.

I have not never seen any of Cassatt's paintings in person. I want to
(27)   (28)

start a club at school called the American impressionist club, whose

members could study these paintings together.

---

11 Rewrite sentence 18 correctly.

She was interested in painting from an early age.

12 In sentence 19, how could studies art best be rewritten?

studied art

GO ON ➡

13 In sentence 20, <u>France and she became</u> is best written—

A France and she become

B France, and she, became

C France and she had become

D As it is written.

14 In sentence 21, <u>Cassatt's paintings</u> is best written—

F Cassatts' paintings

G Cassatt paintings'

H Cassatts' painting

J As it is written.

15 In sentence 24, <u>in their paintings</u> is best written—

A in her paintings

B in they paintings

C in paintings of theirs

D As it is written.

16 In sentence 26, <u>As a result many</u> is best written—

F As a result, many

G As a result, many,

H As a result many,

J As it is written.

17 In sentence 27, <u>I have not never seen</u> is best written—

A I had not never seen

B I have never seen

C I haven't never seen

D As it is written.

18 In sentence 28, the <u>American impressionist club</u> is best written—

F The American Impressionist club

G the american impressionist club

H the American Impressionist Club

J As it is written.

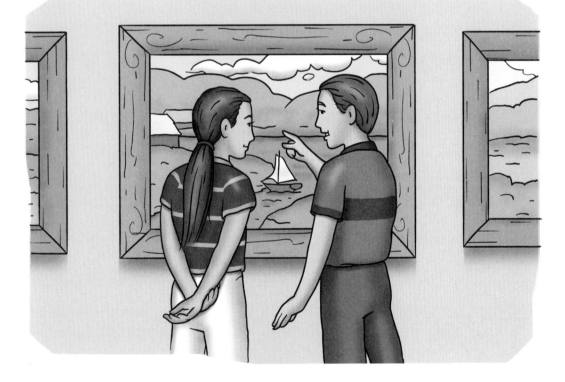

GO ON

Answers

13 Ⓐ Ⓑ ● Ⓓ   15 ● Ⓑ Ⓒ Ⓓ   17 Ⓐ ● Ⓒ Ⓓ

14 Ⓕ Ⓖ Ⓗ ●   16 ● Ⓖ Ⓗ Ⓙ   18 ● Ⓖ Ⓗ Ⓙ

For questions 19–30, read each sentence carefully. If one of the words is misspelled, darken the circle for that word. If all of the words are spelled correctly, then darken the circle for *No mistake*.

19   It is <u>uncommen</u> for Gina to turn in an <u>incomplete</u> <u>assignment</u>. <u>No mistake</u>
        A   **B**   **C**   **D**

20   We had a <u>great</u> time at the <u>amusment</u> park <u>yesterday</u>. <u>No mistake</u>
            F   **G**   **H**   **J**

21   The lead <u>karacter</u> in the <u>play</u> wore a <u>cape</u>. <u>No mistake</u>
           A   **B**   **C**   **D**

22   Hiroshi was <u>assessed</u> a fine <u>because</u> of his <u>overdo</u> books. <u>No mistake</u>
                F   **G**   **H**   **J**

23   The <u>chemist</u> <u>analyzed</u> the sample in the <u>laboratory</u>. <u>No mistake</u>
        A   **B**   **C**   **D**

24   The <u>cinnamon</u> bear was <u>hibernateing</u> during the <u>winter</u> months. <u>No mistake</u>
          F   **G**   **H**   **J**

25   I want to <u>acknowledge</u> all of the hard work <u>involved</u> in this <u>project</u>. <u>No mistake</u>
            A   **B**   **C**   **D**

26   Our <u>basketball</u> team plays <u>tonight</u> in the <u>semefinal</u> game. <u>No mistake</u>
         F   **G**   **H**   **J**

27   The <u>professor</u> <u>specifyed</u> that the exam <u>should</u> last for one hour. <u>No mistake</u>
        A   **B**   **C**   **D**

28   Queen Victoria <u>rained</u> over the <u>British</u> Empire for sixty-four <u>years</u>. <u>No mistake</u>
              F   **G**   **H**   **J**

29   That <u>document</u> is <u>written</u> in <u>eraseable</u> ink. <u>No mistake</u>
        A   **B**   **C**   **D**

30   The <u>dangerous</u> old <u>building</u> was <u>condemed</u> by the city. <u>No mistake</u>
        F   **G**   **H**   **J**

STOP

Answers

19 Ⓐ Ⓑ Ⓒ Ⓓ	22 Ⓕ Ⓖ Ⓗ Ⓙ	25 Ⓐ Ⓑ Ⓒ Ⓓ	28 Ⓕ Ⓖ Ⓗ Ⓙ
20 Ⓕ Ⓖ Ⓗ Ⓙ	23 Ⓐ Ⓑ Ⓒ Ⓓ	26 Ⓕ Ⓖ Ⓗ Ⓙ	29 Ⓐ Ⓑ Ⓒ Ⓓ
21 Ⓐ Ⓑ Ⓒ Ⓓ	24 Ⓕ Ⓖ Ⓗ Ⓙ	27 Ⓐ Ⓑ Ⓒ Ⓓ	30 Ⓕ Ⓖ Ⓗ Ⓙ

READING COMPREHENSION

Use the removable answer sheet on page 127 to record your answers for the practice tests.

Sample A

Bill looks forward to spring because he plays baseball. During fall and winter, however, he has to sell calendars. The money from the calendar sales pays for his uniform.

What does Bill do before he plays baseball?

A practices at the batting cages

B sells calendars

C shops for a uniform

D makes his uniform

STOP

For questions 1–26, carefully read each selection. Then darken the circle for the correct answer.

All About Insects

Did you know that there are more than 800,000 species of insects in the world? A few hundred of these are harmful pests. Insects annually destroy more than ten percent of the crops raised in the United States. The worst of these crop pests include Colorado beetles, chinch bugs, and grasshoppers. Colorado beetles damage potatoes, while chinch bugs destroy corn and other crops. Swarms of grasshoppers can completely destroy fields of crops.

Insects can cause other damage. Moths and beetles damage fabrics; flies, ants, and cockroaches spoil food; and termites damage furniture and the structures of buildings.

Harmful pests cause disease and other health problems. Fleas and lice cause pain and tissue damage, and flies can carry germs that cause cholera and typhoid fever. Some insects transmit deadly diseases, such as African sleeping sickness and malaria.

The number of helpful species of insects far outweighs the number of harmful species. Helpful insects include butterflies, moths, bees, flies, and wasps. These insects pollinate fruit trees, vegetables, and flowering plants. Some insects provide products. Honeybees make honey and beeswax. Silk moths produce silk. Other helpful insects feed on destructive insects. Ladybugs eat aphids—insects that damage flowering and food plants.

Perhaps the most important insects are those that serve as a food source. A number of plants, birds, reptiles, and fish eat insects as the main part of their diet. *Entomologists* have discovered about 500 species of insects that people use as a food source. Insects are high in protein, minerals, and vitamins. They are part of the diet of people living in Asia, Africa, and South America. For example, giant water bugs are popular in Asia. In South America, some people buy a species of ant as a treat in movie theaters. In Japan, insect farmers harvest wasps to be cooked, canned, and sold. Today some people in the United States eat fried caterpillars and chocolate-covered bees and ants.

GO ON

1   Which insects are considered to be both harmful and helpful?

   A   flies

   B   boll weevils

   C   fleas

   D   lice

2   Which insect is responsible for carrying germs that cause typhoid fever?

   F   Colorado beetles

   G   grasshoppers

   H   fleas

   J   flies

3   According to the selection, how many species of insects are there in the world?

   A   more than 800,000

   B   a few hundred thousand

   C   500

   D   a few hundred

4   Insects are an important part of the diet of people in Asia, Africa, and South America because insects are high in—

   F   vitamins.

   G   fats.

   H   germs.

   J   calories.

5   This selection was most likely written in order to—

   A   describe the harmful and beneficial effects of insects.

   B   encourage agriculture around the world.

   C   promote the use of silk products.

   D   explain the many ways to prepare insects for meals.

6   The web shows some important ideas in the selection.

   Which of these belongs in the empty space?

   F   cause disease

   G   eaten as treats in theaters

   H   produce silk

   J   eat other insects

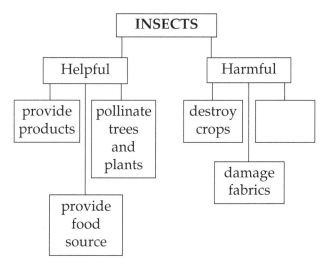

7   What is an *entomologist*?

_____

_____

_____

_____

_____

_____

8   What service do ladybugs provide?

_____

_____

_____

_____

_____

_____

GO ON➡

The History of Chewing Gum

Do you like chewing gum? Millions of people around the world do. It's difficult to imagine a place where people don't chew gum. Chewing gum has been taken up the highest mountain peaks, deep down into the oceans, and even into space.

Chewing gum has been in existence for a long time. It was first enjoyed by the ancient Greeks about A.D. 50. They chewed the sap of the mastic tree. The Mayans of Central America chewed chicle, the resin of the sapodilla tree. When the pilgrims came to North America, Native Americans gave them the resin of spruce trees to chew.

In 1848 John Curtis of Maine manufactured the first gum for sale. The gum sold so well that Curtis built the world's first gum factory and hired 200 workers. In 1906 Frank Fleer came up with the idea of bubble gum. He called his gum Blibber-Blubber, but it was never sold. It was so sticky that if it got on the skin, a person had to scrub it with *turpentine,* or paint thinner, to remove it.

In 1926 the first successful bubble gum, Dubble Bubble, was invented by an accountant at a gum company. As he watched the first batch being made, he realized that it had no color. He grabbed the only coloring around—pink. The gum became so popular that most bubble gum today is still pink.

Let's take a look at how gum is made. There must be a base to make the gum sticky. This base is usually a combination of natural and *synthetic* products. The natural base is made from latex. Latex is the sap that flows in certain trees found in the rain forest. First, the ingredients for the base are mixed together. They are heated to a high temperature and a thick syrup is formed. The syrup is poured into a giant mixer that can hold up to a ton of ingredients. Natural or sugar-free sweeteners are added to make the gum sweet and moist. Then flavorings are added according to the recipe being used.

When the gum comes out of the mixers, it looks like bread dough. It is deposited on belts where it cools. From there it goes to machines that knead it. It is kneaded for a few hours, then cut into rectangular chunks.

If the dough is going to become sheet gum, it is then sent through large rollers that flatten it into thin sheets. The large sheets are cut into small sticks. The sticks are wrapped and sealed. To make bubble gum, the dough is squeezed through a tube. Then it is cut into small balls and wrapped. Finally the gum is ready to be shipped to a store and sold.

Now you know a little about the history of chewing gum and how it is made. But there are many other interesting facts about gum. For example, a dentist in Oregon once helped solve a murder by examining a piece of chewing gum. The suspect said he had never been at the scene of the crime. But his saliva and bite marks on a piece of chewing gum found at the crime scene proved he was not telling the truth.

GO ON ➡

9 People who choose to read this selection are probably interested in—

A participating in sports.

B the history of inventions.

C learning accounting methods.

D marketing products.

10 The boxes show some directions for making gum.

The base is made. 1	Sweeteners are added. 2	The gum is kneaded. 3	4

Which of these belongs in Box 4?

F Flavorings are added.

G The gum is cut into rectangles.

H The gum is wrapped.

J The gum is shipped to stores.

11 Blibber-Blubber was never sold because—

A it was too expensive to buy.

B it was too sticky.

C it was not the right color.

D it was too difficult to make.

12 You can tell the word *turpentine* in this selection means—

F paint thinner.

G soap.

H clothes detergent.

J grease.

13 Where was gum first chewed?

A in Central America

B in North America

C in ancient Greece

D in Maine

14 A recipe is used for each kind of gum—

F so that the person making it will not forget to mix the ingredients.

G because the owner of the company requires it.

H so that the gum will taste the same each time it is made.

J so that sticks of gum will always look the same.

15 You can tell the word *synthetic* means—

A necessary.

B tinted.

C manufactured.

D foreign.

16 What is used to make the base of chewing gum?

F sweeteners

G natural and synthetic products

H flavorings

J flour

17 Why is most bubble gum pink?

A It is illegal to make it any other color.

B Other colors do not stick to the gum as well as pink does.

C Only pink makes good bubbles.

D The first bubble gum was pink and it was very popular.

18 What is the main idea of the last paragraph?

_____

_____

_____

_____

_____

GO ON➡

Sharon's Birthday Dinner

In Sharon's family, each family member gets to choose his or her favorite birthday meal. Here are the recipes used for Sharon's birthday dinner.

Stuffed Shrimp Appetizer

Ingredients:

cooked shrimp, large to jumbo

chives, chopped

cream cheese

shrimp sauce

With a knife, split large-to-jumbo size shrimp open down the back, but not all the way through. Mix chopped chives and cream cheese together. Stuff shrimp with mixture and secure with a toothpick. Pour shrimp sauce, to taste, over shrimp. Refrigerate for one hour before serving.

Sweet and Sour Salad

Ingredients:

4 cups fresh broccoli or cauliflower, cut into bite-size pieces

8 slices bacon, cooked crisp and crumbled

1 small red onion, chopped

3 tablespoons cider vinegar

1 cup mayonnaise

$\frac{1}{4}$ cup sugar

Pour broccoli into bowl with onion and crumbled bacon. Mix cider vinegar, mayonnaise, and sugar and pour over vegetables. Refrigerate at least a few hours, but overnight is better.

Swiss Chicken Cutlets

Ingredients:

5 chicken cutlets

1 egg, beaten

1 cup bread crumbs

$\frac{1}{4}$ cup oil

$\frac{1}{4}$ cup flour

$\frac{1}{8}$ teaspoon pepper

3 tablespoons butter or margarine

1 teaspoon salt

$2\frac{1}{3}$ cups milk

1 cup (8 ounces) shredded Swiss cheese

Pound chicken cutlets with mallet. Sprinkle chicken cutlets with salt and dip in beaten egg. Then cover chicken cutlets with bread crumbs. In a frying pan or skillet, brown the breaded chicken cutlets. Set aside.

In a skillet, melt butter and blend in flour, salt, pepper, and milk. Cook mixture until thickened. Remove mixture from heat. Pour half the mixture into a baking pan. Arrange chicken cutlets on top. Then pour the remaining mixture over the chicken cutlets. Sprinkle the Swiss cheese on top. Bake in the oven at 350°F for 50 minutes.

GO ON

19 In the recipe for stuffed shrimp, the phrase "not all the way through" means—

F partially cook the shrimp.

G cut the shrimp part of the way without cutting it into two halves.

H refrigerate the shrimp before cooking.

J mix together only half the chives and cream cheese.

20 What do you need in order to make the appetizer?

A a measuring spoon

B a grater

C a knife

D a baking pan

21 What could be substituted for broccoli in the Sweet and Sour Salad?

F bacon

G red onion

H cauliflower

J chives

22 If you didn't have a mallet for the chicken recipe, you could use—

A a can opener.

B a heavy wooden spoon.

C a measuring cup.

D a baking pan.

23 Another good name for "Swiss Chicken Cutlets" is—

F "Spinach Noodles with Chicken."

G "Breaded Chicken and Cheese."

H "Chicken and Potato Bake."

J "Chicken in Mushroom Gravy."

24 What two ingredients in the salad recipe make the dish "sweet and sour?"

_____

_____

_____

_____

25 You need all the following to make the Swiss Chicken Cutlets *except*—

A an egg beater.

B a measuring spoon.

C a skillet.

D a spatula.

26 What step needs to be done just before baking the chicken?

_____

_____

_____

_____

_____

_____

STOP

Sample A

Something that is <u>reinforced</u> is—

A purchased

B strengthened

C burned

D emptied

For questions 1–9, darken the circle for the word or group of words that has the same or almost the same meaning as the underlined word.

1 An <u>autograph</u> is—

A a photograph

B an address

C a telephone number

D a signature

2 A <u>haven</u> is a—

F safe place

G landing field

H hospital

J busy highway

3 A person who is <u>valiant</u> is—

A meek

B wealthy

C weak

D courageous

4 Something that is <u>revised</u> is—

F altered   H interrupted

G composed   J interpreted

5 To <u>singe</u> is to—

A chop finely   C laugh loudly

B scrub harshly   D burn slightly

6 A <u>petition</u> is a kind of—

F charity   H poison

G request   J conference

7 A <u>grievance</u> is a—

A funeral   C complaint

B pain   D sadness

8 To <u>administer</u> is to—

F manage   H neglect

G play   J mismanage

9 Something that is <u>fictitious</u> is—

A heroic   C adventurous

B imaginary   D real

Sample B

> She took a <u>direct</u> flight to Denver.

In which sentence does <u>direct</u> have the same meaning as it does in the sentence above?

A This is the most <u>direct</u> route home.

B Mr. Arnold will <u>direct</u> the choir.

C He is a <u>direct</u> descendant of George Washington.

D Could you <u>direct</u> me to the library?

STOP

For questions 10–14, darken the circle for the sentence in which the underlined word means the same as it does in the sentence in the box.

10

> The school board will discuss that <u>issue</u> tonight.

In which sentence does <u>issue</u> have the same meaning as it does in the sentence above?

F Where is the March <u>issue</u> of this magazine?

G The city's attorney will <u>issue</u> a statement.

H Recycling is a very important <u>issue</u>.

J The sergeant will <u>issue</u> clean uniforms in an hour.

11

> Karl ran the last <u>lap</u> of the relay race.

In which sentence does <u>lap</u> have the same meaning as it does in the sentence above?

A The kitten began to <u>lap</u> the milk.

B Ryan held the baby gently in his <u>lap</u>.

C The horse stumbled during the third <u>lap</u> of the race.

D The waves began to <u>lap</u> against the side of the boat.

12

> Do you know how to <u>prune</u> that tree?

In which sentence does <u>prune</u> have the same meaning as it does in the sentence above?

F Amanda refused to eat the <u>prune</u>.

G Jenna would have to <u>prune</u> the budget before it would get approved.

H <u>Prune</u> away the extra decorations, please.

J If you <u>prune</u> the bush, it will have more abundant fruit next year.

13

> That dress will <u>appeal</u> to her.

In which sentence does <u>appeal</u> have the same meaning as it does in the sentence above?

A The mayor will <u>appeal</u> to the citizens of the city to remain calm in the crisis.

B The attorney will <u>appeal</u> the case to a higher court.

C Does that restaurant <u>appeal</u> to you?

D I will <u>appeal</u> to her to go with me.

14

> You need to draw two <u>parallel</u> lines.

In which sentence does <u>parallel</u> have the same meaning as it does in the sentence above?

F Rita's career seems to <u>parallel</u> that of her mother's.

G Hiking through the beautiful mountainside has no <u>parallel</u>.

H Please park your car between the <u>parallel</u> stripes on the pavement.

J The twins have <u>parallel</u> interests.

GO ON

Sample C

Khalid acted as host and <u>conducted</u> our monthly meeting. <u>Conducted</u> means—

A discovered

B vacationed

C directed

D stored

STOP

For questions 15–22, darken the circle for the word or words that give the meaning of the underlined word.

15 The king issued a <u>proclamation</u> stating that everyone in the kingdom had to pay the new tax. <u>Proclamation</u> means—

A report

B law

C announcement

D letter

16 Jill was upset because the same dream was <u>recurring</u> every night. <u>Recurring</u> means—

F repeating

G shining

H ringing

J matching

17 She treated him with <u>disdain</u>. <u>Disdain</u> means—

A respect

B scorn

C great care

D anger

18 The police assured her that it was merely a <u>routine</u> investigation. <u>Routine</u> means—

F short

G serious

H regular

J prison

19 His <u>pompous</u> behavior embarrasses everyone. <u>Pompous</u> means—

A modest

B arrogant

C simple

D polite

20 There was an <u>urgency</u> in her voice that made us worry. <u>Urgency</u> means—

F harsh edge

G demand for immediate action

H lack of depth

J legal decision

21 She had a <u>sedentary</u> job that required little travel. <u>Sedentary</u> means—

A energetic

B inactive

C active

D exciting

22 Because she ran a red light, Rachel was held <u>liable</u> for the car accident. <u>Liable</u> means—

F innocent

G exempt

H insensitive

J responsible

STOP

Sample A

What is the value of the 6 in 273.0462?

A   6 hundredths

B   6 thousandths

C   6 ten-thousandths

D   6 millionths

STOP

For questions 1–47, darken the circle for the correct answer, or write in the answer.

1   After picking raspberries, 4 people compared the amounts of berries in their buckets. Juan's bucket was $\frac{2}{3}$ full. Jamie's was $\frac{4}{5}$ full, Barb's was $\frac{1}{2}$ full, and Hazel's was $\frac{3}{8}$ full. How would these amounts be arranged if they were listed in order from greatest to least amount?

A $\frac{2}{3}, \frac{3}{8}, \frac{4}{5}, \frac{1}{2}$

B $\frac{4}{5}, \frac{2}{3}, \frac{1}{2}, \frac{3}{8}$

C $\frac{1}{2}, \frac{3}{8}, \frac{4}{5}, \frac{2}{3}$

D $\frac{3}{8}, \frac{1}{2}, \frac{2}{3}, \frac{4}{5}$

2   Six hours ago the temperature in Fargo, North Dakota, was -23°. Since then, the temperature has risen 20 degrees. What is the current temperature?

_____

3   What is the value of point C on the number line?

F $2\frac{1}{3}$ H $3\frac{2}{3}$

G $\frac{1}{3}$ J   4

4   One estimate for the distance from Earth to the Andromeda Galaxy is 2,300,000 light years. What is this distance expressed in scientific notation?

A 2.3×10^5 C 2.3×10^6

B 23×10^5 D 2.3×10^7

5   If a cave explorer enters a cave at ground level, follows a passage to 45 feet underground, then takes a turn and follows a passage back up 23 feet, where would the person be, relative to ground level?

F   68 feet   H   -22 feet

G   34 feet   J   -45 feet

6   Which fraction is *not* equivalent to the others in the group?

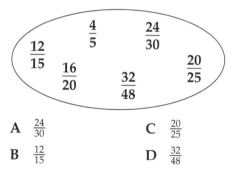

A $\frac{24}{30}$ C $\frac{20}{25}$

B $\frac{12}{15}$ D $\frac{32}{48}$

7   Matt mowed $\frac{5}{8}$ of the lawn and then stopped to eat lunch. What percent of the lawn has been mowed?

F   58.5%   H   67.5%

G   62.5%   J   87.5%

GO ON

8 Four friends wanted to share a pizza. The basic price for a plain cheese pizza is $8.75. Each additional topping costs $0.75. The friends ordered a pizza with pepperoni, mushrooms, and onions. Which expression shows what each person paid?

A $\frac{8.75}{4} + \frac{75}{3}$

B $8.75 \div 4 + \frac{(3 \times 0.75)}{4}$

C $\frac{(8.75 + 0.75)}{4}$

D $(3 \times 4) + (8.75 + 0.75)$

9 Which of the scales shown here is correctly balanced?

F

G

H

J

10 Which symbol makes this statement true?

7 yards___ 7 meters

A >

B <

C =

D ≥

11 Which decimal represents the shaded part of the figure?

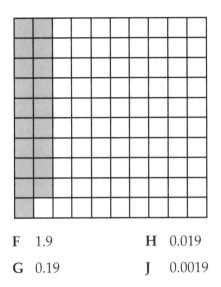

F   1.9   H   0.019

G   0.19   J   0.0019

12 The sum of two numbers is 68. One of the numbers is 14 less than the other number. Which of the following equations could be used to find the two numbers?

A $\frac{68}{n} = n + 14$

B $68 = n + (n - 14)$

C $68 \div 14 = n + n$

D $68n = n + 14$

13 Which block is in the wrong group?

Primes   Composites

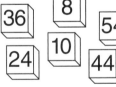

F   61

G   44

H   27

J   8

GO ON➡

14 Last weekend, Gary and Carol collected aluminum cans for recycling. The expression $g = \frac{c}{2}$ shows the relationship between the number of cans Gary (g) collected and the number of cans Carol (c) collected. If Gary collected 438 cans, how many did Carol collect?

A 219

B 336

C 657

D 876

15 A group of hikers planned to take 4 days to climb to the top of a mountain that is 9,753 feet high. The first night they camped $\frac{2}{3}$ of the way up the mountain. Which expression could be used to find D, the distance they had left to reach the top of the mountain?

F $D = (9{,}753 \div 4) \times 2$

G $D = (1 - \frac{2}{3}) + 9{,}753$

H $D = 9{,}753 \div (4 - \frac{2}{3})$

J $D = 9{,}753 - (\frac{2}{3} \times 9{,}753)$

16 Fill in the numbers in Row 6.

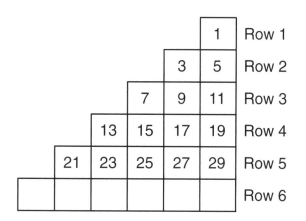

17 In the table below, find the missing value of x for the given function.

x	$\frac{x}{6} + 2$
3	$2\frac{1}{2}$
12	
0	2
	14
-6	1

A 2, 36

B 4, 72

C 6, 24

D 6, 48

18 The graph shows the results of the recent city council elections. If 330,000 people voted, how many people voted for Martinez?

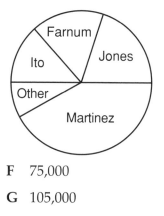

F 75,000

G 105,000

H 180,000

J 250,000

19 In a recent marshmallow-eating contest, the winner ate 30 marshmallows in 5 minutes. At that rate, how many marshmallows would the winner eat if the contest lasted 20 minutes?

_____

_____

_____

GO ON ➡

Use the graph below to answer question 20.

GASES AND CHEMICALS EMITTED INTO THE AIR

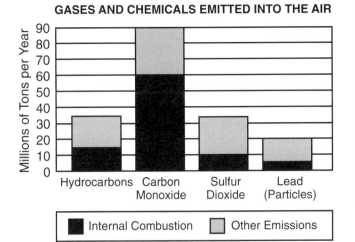

20 What can be concluded from the information in the graph?

A Gases enter the air through three main sources.

B Internal combustion engines release millions of tons of gases and chemicals into the air.

C More lead particles than chemicals are present in the air.

D Relatively few gases and chemicals are present in the air.

21 If digits cannot be repeated, how many 3-digit numbers can be formed using only the digits 3, 5, 6, 8, and 9?

F 5   H 36

G 24   J 60

22 The scatter plot below shows the number of students in each class in a certain school.

School Population

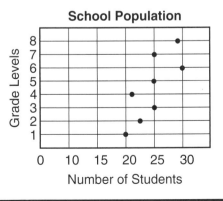

According to the scatter plot, how many students are in the eighth grade?

_____

_____

_____

_____

Use the chart below to answer question 23.

Weekly Reading Chart	
Hours	Number of Students
1	6
2	12
3	18
4	4

23 What is the average (mean) amount of time spent reading each week by this group?

_____

_____

_____

_____

24 A bag contains 10 colored cubes. Without looking into the bag, Richard drew out a cube and then replaced it in the bag. He did this 10 times and recorded the results in the table shown here. What conclusion can be drawn from this information?

Blue	Red	Yellow
7	1	2

A There is an equal number of blue, red, and yellow cubes in the bag.

B There are probably more blue cubes than other colors of cubes.

C There are only three colors of cubes in the bag.

D There are more than three colors of cubes in the bag.

GO ON➡

John Eagle Feather took a survey of his class and made a frequency table showing the number of hours his classmates spent on homework each night. Use the table to answer questions 25 though 27.

Number of Hours Spent on Homework
2 2 3 1 1 1 0 3 2 0 4 2 1 3 1 1 2 2 2 3

25 According to the table, how many students were included in the survey?

_____

_____

_____

_____

26 Which tally chart shows the number of students who spent less than 3 hours doing homework?

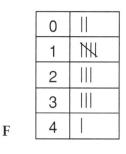

0	II
1	NN
2	III
3	III
4	I

F

0	III
1	IIII
2	NN
3	III
4	III

H

0	III
1	IIII
2	II
3	NN
4	II

G

0	II
1	NN I
2	NN II
3	IIII
4	II

J

27 What is the probability that a student spent 1 hour on homework?

A $\frac{2}{5}$

B $\frac{3}{5}$

C $\frac{3}{20}$

D $\frac{3}{10}$

28 Which figure below has the same number of faces as the figure shown here?

F

G

H

J

29 How much gravel would be needed to fill 75% of the container shown here?

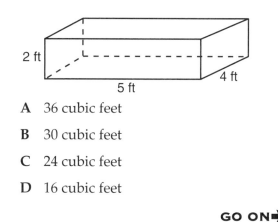

2 ft

5 ft

4 ft

A 36 cubic feet

B 30 cubic feet

C 24 cubic feet

D 16 cubic feet

GO ON

30 The face of a wrist watch has a diameter of 28 millimeters. What is its approximate circumference?
(Use $C = 2\pi r$ and $\pi = 3.14$.)

   F 44 millimeters

   G 88 millimeters

   H 615 millimeters

   J 2461 millimeters

31 Which figure shows the result of rotating the tennis shoe 180°?

32 Which coordinates best represent the last point needed to complete the vertices of a rectangle?

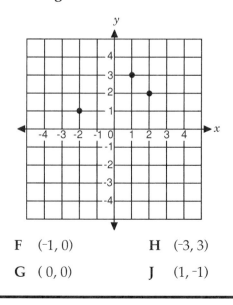

   F (-1, 0)   **H** (-3, 3)

   G (0, 0)   **J** (1, -1)

33 The figure shows the circular path covered by a lawn sprinkler. What is the approximate area covered by the sprinkler? (Use $A = \pi r^2$ and $\pi = 3.14$.)

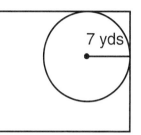

   A 154 square yards

   B 128 square yards

   C 65 square yards

   D 49 square yards

34 In the figure shown here, P is the center of the circle. The line segments are 3 centimeters and 4 centimeters long. What is the diameter of the circle?

   F 1.5 centimeters

   G 3 centimeters

   H 6 centimeters

   J 7 centimeters

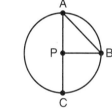

35 Which of these numbers has no line segments that are parallel?

11 14
12 77

_____

_____

_____

_____

GO ON➡

Television station WSTB in Clear Valley broadcasts within a 150-mile range.

Use your inch ruler to help answer question 36.

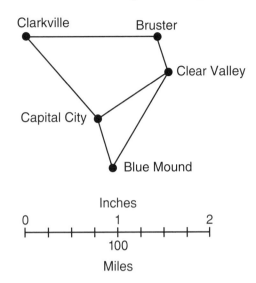

Inches

0   1   2

100

Miles

36   **Which town or towns can receive WSTB's television broadcasts?**

A   Blue Mound only

B   Bruster and Blue Mound only

C   Capital City, Bruster, and Blue Mound only

D   Clarkville, Capital City, Bruster, and Blue Mound

37   **Use your centimeter ruler to answer this question. What is the area of this triangle? (Use $A = \frac{1}{2}bh$.)**

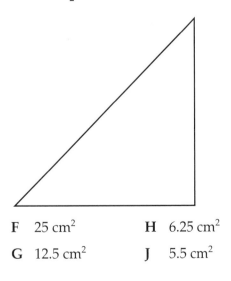

F   25 cm²   H   6.25 cm²

G   12.5 cm²   J   5.5 cm²

38   **The McGill's electric bill varies between $77 and $84 a month. What would be the best estimate of their electric bill for the next 11 months?**

A $80

B $100

C $800

D $1,000

39   **Patty hiked 5,600 meters around the lake. How many kilometers did Patty hike?**

F   0.560

G   5.6

H   56

J   560

40   **Which is closest to the measure of the angle formed by Main Street and First Street?**

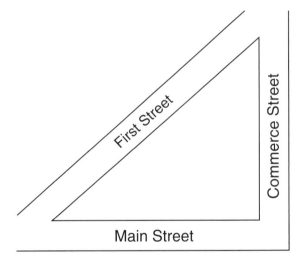

A   10°

B   45°

C   90°

D   130°

GO ON➡

41 A model car is built on a scale of 1 centimeter = 0.25 meters. If the actual car is 4.5 meters long, how long is the model?

F 18 centimeters

G 29.5 centimeters

H 45 centimeters

J 45.5 centimeters

42 Of the 40 members of the school track team, 45% are in the seventh and eighth grades, 35% are in the sixth grade, and 20% are in the fifth grade. How many members are in the sixth grade?

A 8

B 14

C 18

D 26

43 Maxine is sailing around the world. She planned for the trip to take 180 days. If she has been sailing for 78 days, what is the best estimate of the number of days remaining?

_____

_____

_____

_____

44 The distance from Campbell Street to the downtown business district is $6\frac{3}{4}$ miles. The distance from Emery Drive to the business district is $\frac{1}{4}$ of that distance. How far is it from Emery Drive to the business district?

F $1\frac{11}{16}$ miles

G $6\frac{1}{2}$ miles

H 7 miles

J 27 miles

45 To raise funds for a special project, the Girls' Athletic Association ordered 450 flowers from a nursery to sell at school. The nursery charged $0.35 each for the daisies and $0.45 each for the carnations. If the sales tax is 7.25%, what other information is needed to find the total cost of the flowers?

A The colors of the flowers

B How many flowers each member is required to sell

C The total number of members in the Girls' Athletic Association

D How many of each kind of flower was ordered

46 The science class collected 5 tomatoes from the plants they grew in the school greenhouse. The weights are listed in the table below. What is the missing weight?

Samples

A	B	C	D	E	Mean
266	127	562		490	359

Weight measured in grams

F 139

G 232

H 350

J 435

47 Isabel's mother was 25 years old when Isabel was born. In 9 years her mother will be twice the age she was when Isabel was born. How old is Isabel?

_____

_____

_____

_____

STOP

Sample A

$213 \times .03 =$

A 0.639
B 6.39
C 63.09
D 639
E NH

STOP

Sample B

Julio can save $12.50 a week from his allowance and paper route. How much money will he have saved after 6 weeks?

F $2.25
G $16.75
H $28
J $75
K NH

STOP

For questions 1–14, darken the circle for the correct answer. Darken the circle for NH (Not Here) if the correct answer is not given. If no choices are given, write in your answer.

1

$\frac{7}{9} - \frac{1}{3} =$

A $\frac{4}{9}$
B 1
C $\frac{2}{3}$
D $1\frac{1}{3}$
E NH

2

$9 + (-15) + 3 =$

F -3
G 3
H -6
J 27
K NH

3

$0.15 \div 0.8 =$

A 0.7
B 0.23
C 0.1875
D 1.875
E NH

4

$\frac{5}{8} \div 8 =$

F $8\frac{2}{3}$
G $6\frac{2}{3}$
H $\frac{5}{48}$
J $\frac{5}{14}$
K NH

5

$11 \times (-9) =$

A 99
B -2
C -20
D -99
E NH

6

$4\frac{2}{3} \times \frac{1}{8} =$

F $4\frac{7}{8}$
G $4\frac{1}{12}$
H $\frac{15}{11}$
J $\frac{2}{3}$
K NH

7

$16 \div \frac{4}{5} =$

A $16\frac{1}{5}$
B $16\frac{4}{5}$
C $12\frac{4}{5}$
D 20
E NH

8

$5\frac{1}{8}$
$+ 3\frac{3}{4}$

F $8\frac{1}{24}$
G $9\frac{1}{3}$
H $8\frac{7}{8}$
J $8\frac{1}{3}$
K NH

GO ON

9 Jane spent 6 hours preparing her research paper. She wrote for $3\frac{1}{2}$ hours and then edited her work for 1 hour. She spent the remaining time typing. How many hours did Jane spend typing?

A $1\frac{1}{2}$ hours

B 2 hours

C $2\frac{1}{2}$ hours

D 3 hours

E NH

10 Myra saved 20% off the price of a pair of shoes that cost $46. How much money did Myra save?

F $2.75

G $5.25

H $7.85

J $9.20

K NH

20% OFF !

11 Lenore saved $2,500 for a down payment on a car. If the down payment turned out to be only $2,165, how much money did she have left?

_____

_____

_____

_____

12 Sheila spent $8.50 on gas to travel 160 miles. How much would she spend to travel 1,200 miles?

_____

_____

_____

13 Paula baby-sat 3 hours on Saturday and 4 hours on Sunday. She earns $4 per hour. How much money did Paula earn in all?

A $11

B $28

C $18

D $16

E NH

14 At the end of the track season, there was only 56% of the original team members left on the girls' varsity track team. What is 56% rounded to the nearest fraction?

F $\frac{2}{5}$

G $\frac{3}{5}$

H $\frac{3}{25}$

J $\frac{1}{2}$

K NH

STOP

Sample A

Ben wants to write a letter to his state senators expressing his opinion about the proposed building of a garbage dump in a wetlands area in his community. Before he writes the letter, he wants to find information about the location of wetlands areas in his state. He should look in—

A a thesaurus.

B the *Readers' Guide to Periodical Literature.*

C an atlas.

D a dictionary.

 STOP

For questions 1–4, darken the circle for the correct answer, or write in your answer.

> Sheila was assigned to write a report about agriculture. She decided to research backyard gardening and use this as the subject of her report.

1 What should Sheila do before she writes her report?

_____

_____

_____

2 Sheila wants to organize her thoughts for her report. Which of the following ideas should be grouped together with choosing a garden site?

A explaining how to use fertilizer

B testing soil for minerals and nutrients

C weeding a garden

D controlling plant disease

3 What would Sheila <u>not</u> want to include in her report?

F a discussion of organic gardening methods

G a chapter on pesticide use

H a description of the types of fertilizers used in large farming operations

J a list of plants grown by local backyard gardeners

4 Sheila wants to find information about the most recently developed hybrids of seeds. Where is the best place for Sheila to look to find this information?

A an encyclopedia

B her science textbook

C a dictionary

D the *Reader's Guide to Periodical Literature*

GO ON

Here are the Table of Contents and Index from a book Sheila found on backyard gardening. Study them carefully. Then answer questions 5–9.

Table of Contents

Index

5 Sheila wanted to find information about growing carrots. All of these pages would be useful <u>except</u>—

F 21

G 22

H 30–31

J 34

6 Which chapter should Sheila read to find information about how to use a hoe when weeding a garden?

A Chapter 1

B Chapter 2

C Chapter 3

D Chapter 4

7 Which chapter should Sheila read to learn about controlling insects in the garden?

F Chapter 3

G Chapter 4

H Chapter 5

J Chapter 6

8 Sheila wanted to write a paragraph about choosing a garden site that had proper drainage. On which pages could she probably find the most useful information on this topic?

_____

_____

_____

9 Which pages would have information on the best time to plant cabbage?

_____

_____

_____

GO ON➡

Here is a rough draft of the first part of Sheila's report. Read the rough draft carefully. Then answer questions 10–16.

Backyard Gardening

How big is my backyard? How much time do I have? What kinds of
(1)   (2)   (3)
vegetables, fruits, and flowers do I like? How much space does each plant
(4)
need to grow properly?

Choosing a site for your garden requires you to identify several things.
(5)
First, you need to find an area that gets plenty of sunshine—about six
(6)
hours of direct sunlight per day. Second, the ground should be fairly level,
(7)
with a slight slope for good drainage. Finally, you need to check to make
(8)
sure that the soil is free of rocks. Third, you need a water source for
(9)
watering your plants in dry weather.

Once you have identified it, measure your site. You need to find
(10)   (11)
out the size of the site. On paper, make a plan of your garden using the
(12)
measurements. Decide what kinds of plants you want to raise and where
(13)
you will plant them. Where you will plant them depends on many things.
(14)
For example, corn in front of beans. When the corn grows tall, you don't
(15)   (16)
want it to shade the beans from the sun. You need to plant cucumbers
(17)
along a fence or a trellis so the vines have a place to climb as they grow.

GO ON➡

10 What is the best way to write sentence 6?

A   In the beginning, you need to find an area that gets plenty of sunshine—about six hours of direct sunlight per day.

B   About six hours of sunlight per day, is the first thing you need to find an area.

C   Once you need to find an area that gets plenty of sunshine—about six hours of direct sunlight per day.

D   As it is written.

11 Which of these sentences could be added after sentence 4?

F   What time do you usually go to bed at night?

G   These are questions you should ask yourself before you plan your backyard garden.

H   Backyard gardening is a worthwhile hobby.

J   What is your favorite sport in the summer?

12 Which sentence needlessly repeats an idea in the previous sentence?

A   10

B   11

C   12

D   13

13 Which sentence is not in the correct place in the report?

F   5

G   6

H   7

J   8

14 What is the best way to write sentence 10?

_____

_____

_____

_____

_____

15 Which group of words is not a complete sentence?

A   13

B   14

C   15

D   16

16 Which of these sentences could be added after sentence 17?

F   Your plants need water every day.

G   You should ask someone to water your plants if you go on vacation.

H   This allows the cucumbers to ripen in the full sun.

J   Fresh carrots from the garden taste good in salads.

GO ON➡

Here is the next part of the rough draft of Sheila's report. This part has certain words and phrases underlined. Read the draft carefully. Then answer questions 17–24.

The proper tools for gardening <u>helped</u> make the job of caring for
(18)

the garden less difficult. Gardening tools can be bought at garage sales
(19)

because they <u>do not never need</u> to be new to be effective. The following
(20)

tools are essential <u>for gardening: a spade a metal rake a hoe wooden

stakes string gardening gloves.</u> Some optional tools include a weeder
(21)

and a cultivator.

Tools must be cared for properly. <u>They, for example, should be</u>
(22)   (23)

cleaned with soap and water and dried with a clean rag. Put the tools
(24)

away, when not in use, in a storage shed, basement, or garage. Lightly
(25)

oil the tools once a month to keep <u>it</u> from rusting.

You can use <u>fertilizers, and watch</u> your garden grow! The <u>United
(26)   (27)

States Backyard Garden Club</u> recommends using organic materials

for the best-tasting vegetables. A <u>compost pile are made up</u> of layers
(28)

of grass clippings, leaves, vegetable peelings, and dead leaves and

flowers. These materials decay and become rich fertilizer without
(29)

costing you any money. Besides, you can never over-fertilize when using
(30)

compost, and using compost helps keep excess fertilizer from running

off into the water system.

GO ON➡

17 In sentence 18, <u>helped</u> is best written—

    A has helped

    B have helped

    C help

    D As it is written.

18 Correctly rewrite sentence 19.

_____

_____

_____

_____

_____

19 Correctly rewrite sentence 20.

_____

_____

_____

_____

_____

20 In sentence 23, <u>They, for example, should</u> is best written—

    F They, for example should

    G For example, they should

    H For example tools should

    J As it is written.

21 In sentence 25, <u>it</u> is best written—

    A them

    B they

    C their

    D As it is written.

22 In sentence 26, <u>fertilizers, and watch</u> is best written—

    F fertilizers and, watch

    G fertilizers and watch

    H fertilizers and watch,

    J As it is written.

23 In sentence 27, <u>United States Backyard Garden Club</u> is best written—

    A United States backyard Garden Club

    B United States Backyard Garden club

    C United States backyard garden club

    D As it is written.

24 In sentence 28, <u>compost pile are made up</u> is best written—

    F composts piles are made up

    G compost piles are made up

    H compost pile is made up

    J As it is written.

GO ON

For questions 25–36, read each sentence carefully. If one of the words is misspelled, darken the circle for that word. If all of the words are spelled correctly, then darken the circle for *No mistake*.

25 The door <u>mekanism</u> is <u>broken</u> and we are <u>locked</u> out. <u>No mistake</u>
             A   **B**   **C**   **D**

26 He <u>carryied</u> the <u>groceries</u> up the <u>stairs.</u> <u>No mistake</u>
       F   **G**   **H** **J**

27 Carmen's <u>vacuum</u> <u>cleaner</u> motor <u>burned</u> out. <u>No mistake</u>
           A   **B**   **C**   **D**

28 It would be <u>desireable</u> if we could <u>leave</u> by <u>midnight.</u> <u>No mistake</u>
             F   **G**   **H**   **J**

29 The <u>aluminum</u> factory <u>produces</u> a great deal of <u>polution.</u> <u>No mistake</u>
       A   **B**   **C**   **D**

30 <u>Rasberries</u> grow best in <u>temperate</u> <u>climates.</u> <u>No mistake</u>
     F   **G**   **H**   **J**

31 Charles felt <u>extremely</u> <u>week</u> following his <u>illness.</u> <u>No mistake</u>
           A   **B**   **C**   **D**

32 We <u>formed</u> a <u>semecircle</u> around the park <u>ranger.</u> <u>No mistake</u>
      F   **G**   **H**   **J**

33 She lives <u>near</u> the <u>boarder</u> between the two <u>countries.</u> <u>No mistake</u>
         A   **B**   **C**   **D**

34 The <u>magician</u> <u>dissappeared</u> right in <u>front</u> of our eyes. <u>No mistake</u>
      F   **G**   **H**   **J**

35 The <u>collection</u> of <u>artifacts</u> was quite <u>inpressive.</u> <u>No mistake</u>
      A   **B**   **C**   **D**

36 The <u>bakeing</u> bread created a <u>pleasant</u> <u>aroma.</u> <u>No mistake</u>
      F   **G**   **H**   **J**

STOP

UNIT 2:
SIX READING SKILLS
p. 12 1. D 2. F 3. C 4. F
p. 13 1. A 2. H 3. large or roomy
p. 14 1. D 2. H 3. ancient two-wheeled horse-drawn vehicles
p. 15 1. C 2. F 3. city
pp. 16–17 1. C 2. G 3. D 4. He exercised, listened to his doctors, and worked hard. 5. B 6. H 7. C 8. The hop, step, and jump was dropped from the list of events in 1906.
p. 18 1. B 2. F 3. B 4. They are curved like a plane's wings and are flat on the bottom.
p. 19 1. B 2. F 3. B 4. Nick made sure that he had all the pieces required before he began assembling the model.
p. 20 1. D 2. J 3. This story mainly talks about how the Marines used Navajo as a code.
p. 21 1. C 2. G 3. The main idea is that dogs are useful.
pp. 22–23 1. B 2. Aspirin started as a trademark and became a common name. 3. G 4. C 5. Acrophobics fear more than falling.
p. 24 1. B 2. H 3. C 4. Typists were slowed down by the arrangement of the keys.
p. 25 1. C 2. F 3. C 4. The entire country was urged to have polio vaccinations.
pp. 26–27 1. C 2. Intermarriages created two new groups—mestizos and mulattos. 3. G 4. B
p. 28 1. D 2. F 3. Janna was an honest person.
p. 29 1. A 2. G 3. C
p. 30 1. A 2. J 3. D 4. The thieves were squirrels and chipmunks.
p. 31 1. The setting is a carousel. 2. C 3. F 4. C 5. The overall mood is one of darkness and sorrow.

p. 32 1. A 2. F 3. A 4. The author thinks that they may provide fun family entertainment.
p. 33 1. B 2. We need to pass laws to control the amount of money people spend running for Congress. 3. J 4. The author blames the press.
p. 34 1. A 2. F 3. B 4. J
p. 35 1. B 2. He became more sure of himself. 3. H 4. She had been wrong about the book, and people did want to read her story.

UNIT 3:
READING COMPREHENSION
pp. 36–45 SA. D 1. B 2. J 3. D 4. H 5. D 6. F 7. C 8. F 9. Answers will vary. 10. The city of Chicago, with its tall buildings. It is built along Lake Michigan. 11. B 12. F 13. B 14. H 15. B 16. G 17. B 18. H 19. B 20. He was having trouble reading. 21. let other students know about the library's programs. 22. J 23. B 24. H 25. C 26. F 27. D 28. F 29. D 30. The last journal entry describes Queen Victoria Park. 31. Answers will vary. 32. F 33. C 34. G 35. D 36. G 37. It is the only dog food that protects against heartworm. 38. B 39. G 40. B 41. "The First Heart Surgeon"
pp. 46–53 SA. D 1. B 2. F 3. This article is about using little-known plants to solved the world's food problems. 4. A 5. F 6. B 7. He leaped onto the stairway. 8. G 9. D 10. F 11. Ballonets help maintain the shape of the envelope. 12. C 13. G 14. A 15. J 16. B 17. J 18. As the human population grows, more forests are cut down to make farms. 19. A 20. H 21. C 22. H 23. C 24. G

25. B 26. J 27. B 28. Most ingredients are cool vegetables. 29. H 30. There was a shortage of paper during World War I. 31. B 32. G

UNIT 4:
READING VOCABULARY
p. 54 SA. D 1. C 2. J 3. C 4. J 5. C 6. F 7. C 8. F 9. C 10. F
p. 55 SA. B 1. D 2. F 3. D 4. H
p. 56 SA. D 1. B 2. H 3. D 4. G 5. B 6. F 7. C 8. F
pp. 57–59 SA. B 1. C 2. J 3. C 4. J 5. A 6. H 7. D 8. F 9. smell SB. B 10. A 11. J 12. D 13. J 14. A SC. A 15. F 16. B 17. F 18. C 19. J 20. C 21. villain 22. clean

UNIT 5:
MATH PROBLEM-SOLVING PLAN
p. 61 **Step 1.** to determine if $50 is enough money for Migdalia's transportation for one week **Step 2.** She takes the bus twice a day, 3 days a week. She drives 2 days a week. The bus costs $48 for 10 one-way trips. The car costs $0.30 per mile. She drives 52 miles a day. **Step 3.** Compute her travel expenses for one week. Compare that value to $50. **Step 4.** Bus trips cost $4.80 each ($48 ÷10). $4.80 x 6 = $28.80. Driving costs $15.50 per day, or $31.20. $28.80 + $31.20 = $60. She does not have enough money set aside. **Step 5.** Yes, because she will spend $60 each week and has set aside only $50.
p. 62 **Step 1.** to estimate what percent of the carpet will be left over **Step 2.** Alberto purchased 30 square yards of carpeting. 1 square yard = 9 square feet **Step 3.** Determine the number of square feet in 30 square yards. Compute the amount of

carpeting needed and the amount left over. **Step 4.** Area of carpeting = 270 sq. ft; area of room = 240 sq. ft. There will be 30 sq. ft. left over, or about 10%. **Step 5.** Yes, because the computations are correct and the reasoning is sound.

UNIT 6:
MATH PROBLEM SOLVING
pp. 63–64 **SA.** A **1.** D **2.** H **3.** A **4.** G **5.** C **6.** 2° **7.** G **8.** B **9.** H **10.** C **11.** H

p. 65 **SA.** D **1.** A **2.** J **3.** D **4.** 12 c = 2,700 **5.** F

p. 66 **SA.** B **1.** 56, 80 **2.** D **3.** G

pp. 67–68 **SA.** B **1.** A **2.** H **3.** D **4.** F **5.** D **6.** H **7.** 4 **8.** 225

pp. 69–70 **SA.** D **1.** A **2.** G **3.** A **4.** 400 cm^3 **5.** J **6.** B **7.** G **8.** A **9.** 94.2 inches

p. 71 **SA.** B **1.** C **2.** H **3.** 250 km

p. 72 **SA.** B **1.** B **2.** G **3.** D **4.** H **5.** D **6.** G

pp. 73–74 **SA.** D **1.** D **2.** J **3.** A **4.** March 9 **5.** F **6.** B **7.** 8 **8.** 12 **9.** F **10.** C **11.** J

pp. 75–81 **SA.** B **1.** D **2.** H **3.** A **4.** H **5.** B **6.** F **7.** A **8.** F **9.** B **10.** F **11.** D **12.** H **13.** D **14.** F **15.** $1,050 **16.** 46 **17.** B **18.** H **19.** 54, 81 **20.** 440 **21.** C **22.** J **23.** A **24.** 25 **25.** J **26.** D **27.** G **28.** C **29.** 5 **30.** 160 cubic inches **31.** G **32.** A **33.** G **34.** D **35.** J **36.** C **37.** F **38.** Oakley **39.** D **40.** J **41.** C **42.** G **43.** A **44.** F **45.** $134

p. 82 **SA.** D **1.** B **2.** H **3.** A **4.** K **5.** C **6.** J

pp. 83–84 **SA.** D **1.** A **2.** H **3.** B **4.** 4 **5.** F **6.** E **7.** H **8.** C **9.** F **10.** $63.70

pp. 85–86 **SA.** B **SB.** J **1.** A **2.** H **3.** B **4.** F **5.** C **6.** K **7.** B **8.** 1/8 **9.** H **10.** C **11.** G **12.** D **13.** F **14.** $12,600

UNIT 7: LANGUAGE
pp. 87–91 **SA.** A **1.** B **2.** F **3.** D **4.** Yesterday, Justin collapsed while running the mile in physical education class. **5.** H **6.** B **7.** I was out of breath, and my lungs were in extreme pain. **8.** F **9.** C **10.** G **11.** C **12.** F **13.** D **14.** G **15.** C **16.** J **17.** B

p. 92 **SA.** B **1.** B **2.** G **3.** A **4.** F **5.** B **6.** H **7.** D **8.** H

pp. 93–98 **SA.** B **1.** B **2.** J **3.** C **4.** an encyclopedia **5.** F **6.** The Impressionists made an effort not to paint what they knew or felt about the subject—just what they saw. **7.** D **8.** H **9.** D **10.** J **11.** From an early age, she was interested in painting. **12.** studied art **13.** D **14.** J **15.** A **16.** F **17.** B **18.** H **19.** A **20.** G **21.** A **22.** H **23.** D **24.** G **25.** D **26.** H **27.** B **28.** F **29.** C **30.** H

UNIT 8:
PRACTICE TEST 1:
READING COMPREHENSION
pp. 99–104 **SA.** B **1.** A **2.** H **3.** A **4.** F **5.** A **6.** F **7.** An entomologist is a scientists who studies insects. **8.** They eat insects that damage flowering and food plants. **9.** B **10.** G **11.** B **12.** F **13.** C **14.** H **15.** C **16.** G **17.** D **18.** A piece of gum once helped to solve a murder. **19.** G **20.** C **21.** H **22.** B **23.** G **24.** sugar and vinegar **25.** D **26.** Sprinkle cheese on top of the cutlets.

UNIT 9:
PRACTICE TEST 2:
READING VOCABULARY
pp. 105–107 **SA.** B **1.** D **2.** F **3.** D **4.** F **5.** D **6.** G **7.** C **8.** F **9.** B **SB.** A **10.** H **11.** C **12.** J **13.** C **14.** H **SC.** C **15.** C **16.** F **17.** B **18.** H **19.** B **20.** G **21.** B **22.** J

UNIT 10:
PRACTICE TEST 3
PART 1:
MATH PROBLEM SOLVING
pp. 108–115 **SA.** B **1.** B **2.** –3° **3.** H **4.** C **5.** H **6.** D **7.** G **8.** B **9.** H **10.** B **11.** G **12.** B **13.** H **14.** D **15.** J **16.** 31; 33; 35; 37; 39; 41 **17.** B **18.** G **19.** 120 **20.** B **21.** J **22.** 28 students **23.** 2 1/2 **24.** B **25.** 20 **26.** J **27.** D **28.** J **29.** B **30.** G **31.** D **32.** F **33.** A **34.** H **35.** 12 **36.** C **37.** G **38.** C **39.** G **40.** B **41.** F **42.** B **43.** 100 days **44.** F **45.** D **46.** H **47.** 16

PART 2: MATH PROCEDURES
pp. 116–117 **SA.** B **SB.** J **1.** A **2.** F **3.** D **4.** K **5.** D **6.** K **7.** D **8.** H **9.** A **10.** J **11.** $335 **12.** $63.75 **13.** B **14.** G

UNIT 11:
PRACTICE TEST 4: LANGUAGE
pp. 118–124 **SA.** C **1.** make a list of topics to include in her report **2.** B **3.** H **4.** D **5.** H **6.** B **7.** J **8.** pages 1-3 **9.** pages 21-23 **10.** D **11.** G **12.** B **13.** J **14.** Once you have identified your site, you need to measure it. **15.** C **16.** H **17.** C **18.** Gardening tools can be bought at garage sales because they do not need to be new to be effective. **19.** …for gardening; a space, a metal rake, a hoe, wooden stakes, string, and gardening gloves. **20.** G **21.** A **22.** G **23.** D **24.** H **25.** A **26.** F **27.** D **28.** F **29.** C **30.** F **31.** B **32.** G **33.** B **34.** G **35.** C **36.** F

Answer Sheet

STUDENT'S NAME

LAST   FIRST   MI

SCHOOL:

TEACHER:

FEMALE ○   MALE ○

BIRTH DATE

MONTH	DAY	YEAR
Jan ○	⓪ ⓪	⓪ ⓪
Feb ○	① ①	① ①
Mar ○	② ②	② ②
Apr ○	③ ③	③ ③
May ○	④	④ ④
Jun ○	⑤	⑤ ⑤
Jul ○	⑥	⑥ ⑥
Aug ○	⑦	⑦ ⑦
Sep ○	⑧	⑧ ⑧
Oct ○	⑨	⑨ ⑨
Nov ○		
Dec ○		

GRADE ④ ⑤ ⑥ ⑦ ⑧

(Name grid columns with bubbles A–Z)

Fill in the circle for each multiple-choice answer. Write the answers to the open-ended questions on a separate sheet of paper.

TEST 1   Reading Comprehension

SA Ⓐ Ⓑ Ⓒ Ⓓ   5 Ⓐ Ⓑ Ⓒ Ⓓ   10 Ⓕ Ⓖ Ⓗ Ⓙ   15 Ⓐ Ⓑ Ⓒ Ⓓ   20 Ⓐ Ⓑ Ⓒ Ⓓ   25 Ⓐ Ⓑ Ⓒ Ⓓ

1 Ⓐ Ⓑ Ⓒ Ⓓ   6 Ⓕ Ⓖ Ⓗ Ⓙ   11 Ⓐ Ⓑ Ⓒ Ⓓ   16 Ⓕ Ⓖ Ⓗ Ⓙ   21 Ⓕ Ⓖ Ⓗ Ⓙ   26 OPEN ENDED

2 Ⓕ Ⓖ Ⓗ Ⓙ   7 OPEN ENDED   12 Ⓕ Ⓖ Ⓗ Ⓙ   17 Ⓐ Ⓑ Ⓒ Ⓓ   22 Ⓐ Ⓑ Ⓒ Ⓓ

3 Ⓐ Ⓑ Ⓒ Ⓓ   8 OPEN ENDED   13 Ⓐ Ⓑ Ⓒ Ⓓ   18 OPEN ENDED   23 Ⓕ Ⓖ Ⓗ Ⓙ

4 Ⓕ Ⓖ Ⓗ Ⓙ   9 Ⓐ Ⓑ Ⓒ Ⓓ   14 Ⓕ Ⓖ Ⓗ Ⓙ   19 Ⓕ Ⓖ Ⓗ Ⓙ   24 OPEN ENDED

TEST 2   Reading Vocabulary

SA Ⓐ Ⓑ Ⓒ Ⓓ   5 Ⓐ Ⓑ Ⓒ Ⓓ   SB Ⓐ Ⓑ Ⓒ Ⓓ   14 Ⓕ Ⓖ Ⓗ Ⓙ   18 Ⓕ Ⓖ Ⓗ Ⓙ

1 Ⓐ Ⓑ Ⓒ Ⓓ   6 Ⓕ Ⓖ Ⓗ Ⓙ   10 Ⓕ Ⓖ Ⓗ Ⓙ   SC Ⓐ Ⓑ Ⓒ Ⓓ   19 Ⓐ Ⓑ Ⓒ Ⓓ

2 Ⓕ Ⓖ Ⓗ Ⓙ   7 Ⓐ Ⓑ Ⓒ Ⓓ   11 Ⓐ Ⓑ Ⓒ Ⓓ   15 Ⓐ Ⓑ Ⓒ Ⓓ   20 Ⓕ Ⓖ Ⓗ Ⓙ

3 Ⓐ Ⓑ Ⓒ Ⓓ   8 Ⓕ Ⓖ Ⓗ Ⓙ   12 Ⓕ Ⓖ Ⓗ Ⓙ   16 Ⓕ Ⓖ Ⓗ Ⓙ   21 Ⓐ Ⓑ Ⓒ Ⓓ

4 Ⓕ Ⓖ Ⓗ Ⓙ   9 Ⓐ Ⓑ Ⓒ Ⓓ   13 Ⓐ Ⓑ Ⓒ Ⓓ   17 Ⓐ Ⓑ Ⓒ Ⓓ   22 Ⓕ Ⓖ Ⓗ Ⓙ

TEST 3 Part 1: Math Problem Solving

SA Ⓐ Ⓑ Ⓒ Ⓓ	9 Ⓕ Ⓖ Ⓗ Ⓙ	17 Ⓐ Ⓑ Ⓒ Ⓓ	25 OPEN ENDED	33 Ⓐ Ⓑ Ⓒ Ⓓ	41 Ⓕ Ⓖ Ⓗ Ⓙ
1 Ⓐ Ⓑ Ⓒ Ⓓ	10 Ⓐ Ⓑ Ⓒ Ⓓ	18 Ⓕ Ⓖ Ⓗ Ⓙ	26 Ⓕ Ⓖ Ⓗ Ⓙ	34 Ⓕ Ⓖ Ⓗ Ⓙ	42 Ⓐ Ⓑ Ⓒ Ⓓ
3 Ⓕ Ⓖ Ⓗ Ⓙ	11 Ⓕ Ⓖ Ⓗ Ⓙ	19 OPEN ENDED	27 Ⓐ Ⓑ Ⓒ Ⓓ	35 OPEN ENDED	43 OPEN ENDED
4 Ⓐ Ⓑ Ⓒ Ⓓ	12 Ⓐ Ⓑ Ⓒ Ⓓ	20 Ⓐ Ⓑ Ⓒ Ⓓ	28 Ⓕ Ⓖ Ⓗ Ⓙ	36 Ⓐ Ⓑ Ⓒ Ⓓ	44 Ⓕ Ⓖ Ⓗ Ⓙ
5 Ⓕ Ⓖ Ⓗ Ⓙ	13 Ⓕ Ⓖ Ⓗ Ⓙ	21 Ⓕ Ⓖ Ⓗ Ⓙ	29 Ⓐ Ⓑ Ⓒ Ⓓ	37 Ⓕ Ⓖ Ⓗ Ⓙ	45 Ⓐ Ⓑ Ⓒ Ⓓ
6 Ⓐ Ⓑ Ⓒ Ⓓ	14 Ⓐ Ⓑ Ⓒ Ⓓ	22 OPEN ENDED	30 Ⓕ Ⓖ Ⓗ Ⓙ	38 Ⓐ Ⓑ Ⓒ Ⓓ	46 Ⓕ Ⓖ Ⓗ Ⓙ
7 Ⓕ Ⓖ Ⓗ Ⓙ	15 Ⓕ Ⓖ Ⓗ Ⓙ	23 OPEN ENDED	31 Ⓐ Ⓑ Ⓒ Ⓓ	39 Ⓕ Ⓖ Ⓗ Ⓙ	47 OPEN ENDED
8 Ⓐ Ⓑ Ⓒ Ⓓ	16 OPEN ENDED	24 Ⓐ Ⓑ Ⓒ Ⓓ	32 Ⓕ Ⓖ Ⓗ Ⓙ	40 Ⓐ Ⓑ Ⓒ Ⓓ	

Part 2: Math Procedures

SA Ⓐ Ⓑ Ⓒ Ⓓ Ⓔ	2 Ⓕ Ⓖ Ⓗ Ⓙ Ⓚ	5 Ⓐ Ⓑ Ⓒ Ⓓ Ⓔ	8 Ⓕ Ⓖ Ⓗ Ⓙ Ⓚ	11 OPEN ENDED	14 Ⓕ Ⓖ Ⓗ Ⓙ Ⓚ
SB Ⓕ Ⓖ Ⓗ Ⓙ Ⓚ	3 Ⓐ Ⓑ Ⓒ Ⓓ Ⓔ	6 Ⓕ Ⓖ Ⓗ Ⓙ Ⓚ	9 Ⓐ Ⓑ Ⓒ Ⓓ Ⓔ	12 OPEN ENDED	
1 Ⓐ Ⓑ Ⓒ Ⓓ Ⓔ	4 Ⓕ Ⓖ Ⓗ Ⓙ Ⓚ	7 Ⓐ Ⓑ Ⓒ Ⓓ Ⓔ	10 Ⓕ Ⓖ Ⓗ Ⓙ Ⓚ	13 Ⓐ Ⓑ Ⓒ Ⓓ Ⓔ	

TEST 4 Language

SA Ⓐ Ⓑ Ⓒ Ⓓ	7 Ⓕ Ⓖ Ⓗ Ⓙ	14 OPEN ENDED	21 Ⓐ Ⓑ Ⓒ Ⓓ	28 Ⓕ Ⓖ Ⓗ Ⓙ	35 Ⓐ Ⓑ Ⓒ Ⓓ
1 OPEN ENDED	8 OPEN ENDED	15 Ⓐ Ⓑ Ⓒ Ⓓ	22 Ⓕ Ⓖ Ⓗ Ⓙ	29 Ⓐ Ⓑ Ⓒ Ⓓ	36 Ⓕ Ⓖ Ⓗ Ⓙ
2 Ⓐ Ⓑ Ⓒ Ⓓ	9 OPEN ENDED	16 Ⓕ Ⓖ Ⓗ Ⓙ	23 Ⓐ Ⓑ Ⓒ Ⓓ	30 Ⓕ Ⓖ Ⓗ Ⓙ	
3 Ⓕ Ⓖ Ⓗ Ⓙ	10 Ⓐ Ⓑ Ⓒ Ⓓ	17 Ⓐ Ⓑ Ⓒ Ⓓ	24 Ⓕ Ⓖ Ⓗ Ⓙ	31 Ⓐ Ⓑ Ⓒ Ⓓ	
4 Ⓐ Ⓑ Ⓒ Ⓓ	11 Ⓕ Ⓖ Ⓗ Ⓙ	18 OPEN ENDED	25 Ⓐ Ⓑ Ⓒ Ⓓ	32 Ⓕ Ⓖ Ⓗ Ⓙ	
5 Ⓕ Ⓖ Ⓗ Ⓙ	12 Ⓐ Ⓑ Ⓒ Ⓓ	19 OPEN ENDED	26 Ⓕ Ⓖ Ⓗ Ⓙ	33 Ⓐ Ⓑ Ⓒ Ⓓ	
6 Ⓐ Ⓑ Ⓒ Ⓓ	13 Ⓕ Ⓖ Ⓗ Ⓙ	20 Ⓕ Ⓖ Ⓗ Ⓙ	27 Ⓐ Ⓑ Ⓒ Ⓓ	34 Ⓕ Ⓖ Ⓗ Ⓙ	